M000107155

STOP.
BACK UP.
GROW.

A Personal Growth Formula
That is as Easy as Falling Down

Paul J. Angelle, Jr., J.D.

Stop. Back Up. Grow
Copyright © 2021 Paul J. Angelle, Jr., J.D. All rights reserved.

No part of this book may be used or reproduced in any manner whatsoever without written permission, except in the case of brief quotations embodied in critical articles and reviews. For more information, e-mail all inquiries to info@ mindstirmedia.com.

Published by Mindstir Media, LLC
45 Lafayette Rd | Suite 181| North Hampton, NH 03862 | USA
1.800.767.0531 | www.mindstirmedia.com

Printed in the United States of America

ISBN-13: 978-1-7370915-5-4

For Dawn

Table of Contents

PREFACE

Throughout this book, I keep coming back to a simple formula. It is as easy as falling down but often difficult for many people to accomplish. Some of us choose to rely on our instincts and confuse that reliance with thinking—it is not. This book, I pray, helps change that process.

The idea hit me like a blunt object to the face in early April 2020. Like millions of people around the world, I was stuck at home to slow the spread of the coronavirus crisis. The concept, on the surface, disguised itself as common-sense self-discipline. However, I sensed there was more to it and realized I was on to something so simple that it would take an entire book to explain—right? Unable to escape the idea, it continued to bounce around inside my disproportionately large head—taunting me, challenging me. I resolved to test it.

Once confident with the gist of the idea, I asked myself what I needed to do to develop, share, and test my newfound simple truth. As elementary as this formula is, it is an idea—and ideas should be shared, especially a simple concept that could help others avoid a lifetime of less. Then my questions became who could write this and who would read it?

This book contains my disturbingly simple idea, and rather than trying to express it so completely to someone else (and undoubtedly be disappointed), I have chosen to start writing. To me, it would be worth the effort.

I think this concept warrants study, testing, critiques, and criticism, but once this idea is out, people will have one less excuse to avoid the growth they have been missing. My working theory is that, if properly applied, there would no longer be anything insurmountable preventing growth.

Assuming this is what you want.

PART I
PREPARE FOR GROWTH

"When the student is ready, the teacher will appear.
When the student is truly ready . . .
the teacher will disappear."

— Tao Te Ching

CHAPTER ONE

What Does Growth Even Mean?

"Without continual growth and progress, such words as improvement, achievement, and success have no meaning."

— Benjamin Franklin

There is something in your way, there is. It is probably not just one thing, but whatever it is, it can be enormous or minuscule. It might be invisible—and it is quite possible you are not even aware of what it is—but it is there, and you know it.

As a species, humans possess an almost universal desire to improve themselves. Self-help books, personal coaches, therapists, and pharmaceutical companies are everywhere, making lots of money with promises to help people quench that desire for improvement. They claim improvement—or "growth"—can involve a lot of hard work: reading, listening, reflecting, feeling, and even experiencing some nasty side effects or addictions. But no one ever says it is impossible. That is bad for business.

Growth can be many things. There are infinite possibilities, and any improvement you can imagine can resemble growth. The key is imagination, and that is an absolute requirement.

Imagine it. Do not simply wish for it, hope for it, or simply want it. One must be able to see exactly what the finished product looks like. If no one knows precisely what success looks like, it is impossible to tell if anyone ever gets there.

Knowing why such growth is wanted is another prerequisite. It is almost as important as knowing what growth looks like. Rationale dictates enthusiasm for the growth and secures its place in the priority hierarchy, which sets the odds for success. The rationale may exist somewhere in the knowledge of what the failure to grow looks like. The why matters.

For the astute reader, this chapter has established much so far. For the purpose of this book, the definition of growth now includes any desired, imaginable improvement with an articulable reason or rationale.

This is big. It is worth an extra step for emphasis because this new definition can not only assist in potential growth, it can set the stage for dominoes of growth to start falling all over the place. Know that if it has not been imagined in detail, it is not yet potential growth. If the reason why is unclear, it is not yet potential growth. It is not necessarily over; there is simply more work to do before one can back into growth.

What if anyone could clumsily back into a single solution to most, if not all, of their problems?

What if a person could remove that which is and has been stunting their growth by simply making a decision to do so, even if they are not sure what it is?

What if everything holding everyone back is related?

And what if personal growth, however defined, is something that has been within reach and within control all along?

This entire book could be summarized in four words. Rather than revealing these magical words, and simultaneously ruining the effectiveness of the work, the secret lesson reveals itself only after completion. This book contains a simple lesson that anyone can apply to anything and everything they do not like about their life or their situation, creating instant improvement—and ultimately, control of whatever it is.

Do you wish you were closer to your spouse?

Do you wish you made more money?

Do you ever wish others would take you more (or less) seriously?

This book has a simple system that, if followed, works.

This system, based on ownership, involves looking hard at your ugliest weaknesses, picking at them, and realizing that what you thought was so hideous and limiting is actually your hidden strength, your superpower.

If a change is overdue, growth is possible, and you are ready—this book and this system can help. It can help an uptight human resources compliance officer to loosen up, an immature used car salesman to get serious, a bookworm to exercise, and a jock to read books.

Whatever people have become in their lives, it was all their choice, and this fact is difficult for many people to swallow. However, anyone can choose to change whenever they are ready, and it can be as easy as backing up. Taking ownership is crucial; actually understanding who they are and why is the first critical step backward.

Humans are capable of so much when it comes to personal development and growth. Moreover, they typically follow through, despite some incredibly perverse priorities.

One would hope that every person in the world wishes for more than they have, and while that might seem selfish, it is not. Maybe it is not the accumulation of stuff, an increase in wealth, or a substantive relationship—but it is something. All too often, people give up on getting what they want, which is fine. . . unless it's not.

Growth, often defined in a psychological sense, is personal development. In such a context, it is that need for enhancement to improve those feelings they hold about themselves of how effectively they live their lives. Personal development, people believe, makes them "better."

Growth as enlightenment can occur in an escape from ignorance through learning. This is often the goal of education, reading, or any type of experimental research.

Growth can describe an increase in influence, power, wealth, or business. This growth sometimes comes at the expense of other types of growth, but if it is what you want, it's often easily measured.

Growth is not just you. Your relationships can grow in number, in strength, and in depth. Relationships driven by purpose have the highest chance for success and further growth.

Just remember that there are many different ways people can grow, but from this book's perspective, growth is growth. Growth, considered positive in most cases, sometimes comes at a cost. Growing pains are a real thing, and few things in life are free. However, rarely are human beings driven to shrink (unless, of course, they are dieting or downsizing—activities, one could argue, require significant growth).

CHAPTER TWO

See the Barricades

"From him who sees no wood for trees
And yet is busie as the bees
From him that's settled on his lees
And speaketh not without his fees."

— John Heywood

This chapter is all about revisiting the very first sentence in the first chapter—no one can deny the fact some obstacle is in their way. (Actually, they could, but they would have to lie to themselves.) Everyone faces multiple obstacles every day, and that is normal. The lights are not always green when you are driving. In fact, don't they tend to all be red when you are in a hurry? In this case, the obstacle appears to be the red light, but it is not: traffic lights are beyond most drivers' control, and any uncontrollable obstacle is simply a variable.

Most everyone has attended a parade or an event where there was some kind of barricade meant to limit traffic or keep people safe. Wikipedia.com defines a barricade as any object or structure that creates an obstacle to control, block passage, or reroute the flow of traffic in some desired direction. In the military, a barricade denotes any improvised field fortification. While it may be illegal to alter or remove them, technically, barricades are controllable. A controllable obstacle is an entirely different kind of variable than an uncontrollable one. That distinction will prove to be important.

To revisit the red light problem, traffic signals are not a barricade (obviously), but they often get the blame. Sometimes it is the traffic situation in general, the other "stupid" drivers, or even poor municipal planning keeping you from arriving someplace on time.

There is a truly controllable barricade rarely mentioned in these situations, and it is painfully obvious to some but lost on others.

It is safe to assume red lights will stop most drivers in a city multiple times on almost every trip. It is also safe to assume there will be multiple drivers creating more traffic than necessary. Moreover, has anyone ever seen a perfectly-planned traffic design?

These are predictable, uncontrollable, and completely expected obstacles. The barricade is the driver's lack of preparation in considering the obviously unavoidable variables that shouldn't be surprising to anyone who has driven more than once.

Employees never explain to their boss that they were late because they failed to give themselves enough time to account for the known uncontrollable obstacles; it has probably never happened. Surely, the boss knows better and, rather than challenge the tardy employee, moves on to other "boss" tasks. It is hard to imagine bosses making excuses based on flawed logic to employees. In most cases, they do not have to—not because they are the boss, but because they are not late, ever. Bosses plan accordingly.

This illustration about barricades, obstacles, and red lights should ignite the observation of an internal difference between growth experienced by bosses and the growth achieved so far by late employees. The growth, or lack thereof, is the best predictor of success there is. Forget about age, luck, experience, education, attractiveness, or even talent. While they are all factors, the ability to grow is the single greatest asset an ambitious worker can possess (assuming the ambition includes becoming the boss).

It all begins and ends with the ability to see barricades. It is easier for some than others, but if growth is the goal, just as with anything, practice improves the odds of success.

The details have a tendency to overwhelm, and sometimes this can obscure the overall situation. Forests are full of trees, but with too much focus placed on the individual trees, the forest becomes invisible. This tendency to allocate an excess of attention to details is at the root of many barricades.

It is usually a good idea, if possible, to take large projects and break them down into smaller tasks. The same is true with growth of any kind, but sometimes the process of breaking that growth down into smaller parts creates silos. The partitions between these silos can often prevent successes and failures from escaping to further the larger objective. Understanding this potential breakdown is the only way mitigation can succeed.

A great example of this could be the simple attempt of an unorganized individual to become better organized. This could be someone who has struggled with organization in the past, and their lack of logistical prowess is a noticeable weakness that has become a theme in multiple failures.

The first step would be to make a decision to become more organized. With that decision made, the picture of what that growth looks like needs to form in the mind. The finished product could simply be the combination of a cleaner, neater workspace, free from clutter; an organized, accessible list of potential tasks to complete; and a centralized, updatable collection of relevant contacts.

These three general ideas would dictate three distinct duties. The first duty would be to straighten up and clean the workspace. Secondly, a simple to-do list should be created. The third duty would be to collect and organize any potentially relevant contacts. This all seems easy enough.

The culmination of the separate duties should build the bridge to the goal of better organization. A potential, and often likely, barricade to success could be in the silos created by the different tasks. During the first process, as this hero is frantically cleaning the desk, important, forgotten contacts will undoubtedly surface in multiple formats. With too much focus on the actual cleaning, the risk exists of these contacts being lost, as the concept of collecting and organizing those contacts belongs to a completely different duty. Then, when the duty to create a to-do list begins, the relevance of contacts to various work-tasks can be skipped because they were not secured. This happened because securing contacts was a separate duty from cleaning a workspace.

This is a simple example of a predictable, controllable barricade. Purposely created by companies, silos focus assets on specific tasks related to the mission of the business.

Communication failures between silos are common, and when teams do not share a common objective, business growth stalls.

For example, imagine a company's engineering team, tasked with perfecting some automated process, discovers an unrelated problem that could have a potentially negative impact on current and future customers. That information is now well-known and understood throughout the silo, but the sales team could still sell the wrong application to a customer. This would be unfortunate, especially considering that the company was aware of the potential issue through engineering. The company had discovered information that could have brought value to the marketplace, but because that information was stuck in an engineering silo, a customer experience could be bad.

Silos exist to grow companies efficiently, but all too often, communication deficiencies between the silos have turned positives into negatives. The same danger exists in the individual's process for growth, as separate tasks become silos. Awareness of this potential barricade allows for better compartmentalization of tasks without the rigid extent of restricting overlap. Silos in business are manageable, which means the same phenomena are manageable for individuals.

Tasks require an alignment of goals, an understanding of different purposes, mission overlap, and a purposeful effort to combine findings. This is no different from managing tasks in a company.

A solid final step in each of the three duties of this hero's mission to get organized should involve the question of whether anything uncovered during the duty is relevant to any of the other duties. This step prevents this barricade.

Another potential barricade would be if any of the duties' goals were competing. If your only duty is to effectively and efficiently clean a desk, a great way to perform this task would involve a large, empty trash can and a sweeping motion that shovels a hundred percent of the junk from the top of the desk into the can.

The goal of a clean desk is accomplished, but what was on the desk? Sometimes relevant contact information, scribbled on business cards or napkins, exists. Could there have been important documents buried with all the trash? This disorganized mass on top of the desk, presumably, ended up there for a reason.

The goals of the individual duties must include the larger goal of growth. If there is any competition between the duties, and one's success comes only at the expense of another, the process lacks synergy and is effectively broken. This is another barricade.

Some growth, blocked by ignorance or the inability to measure value to ensure proper prioritization, fails to occur. This happens all the time in businesses when owners and employees do not know their numbers. Decisions made on instincts, thoughts, and feelings are sometimes good decisions, but decisions made on relevant and accurate data produce positive, desired results.

Let us assume the workspace in question is actually an elaborate instrument panel inside a remote outpost in Antarctica, and there is zero human contact. Prioritizing the presentable neatness of the workspace, or a huge focus on fashionable clothing, or tasteful conversation pieces over equipment maintenance, rations, and warm clothing might demonstrate a severe lack of awareness. This could be a huge problem. As a rule, focusing on aspects that do little to further a goal indicates an ignorance of what actually influences success. This is another barricade.

Other elements can block growth. Some are predictable, some are not. Developing discernment to identify those manageable barricades, or even predict them, is a key to successful growth. Being able to distinguish between unavoidable obstacles and manageable barricades is the bridge to ownership. The lack of ownership is the largest obstacle to overcome in any situation.

Countless books focus on pushing through barricades or removing obstacles, and they are of great benefit to anyone wishing to grow. The measure of determination within the individual seeking growth is one of the best predictors of success against any foreseeable obstacle. That measure, mortally weakened when fault assigns elsewhere, inevitably evaporates.

Those determined to grow must first position themselves to own any problem before there can be any expectation of an effective solution. Accepting ownership or fault for any barricade is a prerequisite to managing it, but one cannot own what one cannot see.

CHAPTER THREE
Challenge Beliefs

"In the province of the mind, what one believes to be true either is true or becomes true."

— John Lilly

Animals come programmed to follow their impulses, which is usually fine because they have maintained their instincts. The human race has evolved; human instincts have been flushed down the toilet and replaced with what humans often assume is reason. Reason is preferable to instincts on most levels, but somehow human impulses have regressed along with human instincts. Contemporary human actions based on impulses have curiously led the species to most, if not all, of its catastrophic failures.

If one would simply go against all impulses experienced in a given day, that day would end up exponentially better than if some Neanderthal would succumb to any and all impulses felt that same day. This makes no sense, but it has everything to do with the numb or non-existent human instincts leftover from a much more primitive time. Instincts, once vital for survival, have been replaced by beliefs. Beliefs are sometimes based on reason and experience but are also often based on bullshit. Usually, it is the latter that often pooh-poohs human goals.

Goals are important. The reason so much content dedicated to the topic of goals exists is simple: if set correctly, goals make it easier for humans to stay on track to get what they want. Goals improve the odds of success in life, and a lack of goals drastically increases the odds of disappointment, lack of fulfillment, and regret.

Napoleon Hill's definition, that most people have heard, is that a goal is simply a dream with a deadline. As terrible a definition as that is, it can be helpful. Even losers have dreams, and maybe if they would implement some system of deadlines, they could be losers no more.

Goals replace broken human instincts and strengthen people's resistance to those dangerously compelling impulses. Anyone with a clearly stated, properly visualized, and reasonably attainable goal knows the answer when asked, "What is your goal?"

Most goal-setters will have visualized what the successful attainment of said goal looks like. If they have, that vision becomes their strength against any impulse that works against their goal. The clearer the vision, the stronger the resistance will be.

Humans are better at answering questions when they are prepared than when they are put on the spot. This applies to internal questions. No one wants to be unsure when they must consider if an impulse is in their best interest, and not having a relevant, visualized goal could lead to the path of least resistance—which is to follow the impulse.

Therapists often explain that change is hard because everyone struggles with two things: habits and beliefs. Habits are those things done to stay comfortable and to minimize anxiety. Habits become routines, and bad habits can create addictions. Millions of people worldwide drink coffee every morning, and millions of those people would be thrown off and irritable if their day somehow started without coffee. Drinking a cup of coffee every morning is an example of a habit. When deprived of habits, people can often feel tense, unsettled, and even sick—their behavior can actually suffer.

Beliefs are more complicated than habits. Humans possess complex belief systems, and it is within those systems that personalities evolve and behaviors or habits are determined. This idea is the basis for which individuals create identities.

It is almost hopeless if a single man complains about not having a girlfriend, but his daily habits include drinking a large amount of vodka and watching porn for hours after work because he believes it reduces stress. To any outsider, it is painfully obvious that his habitual patterns are working against the likelihood of his complaints ever ending. He may have a goal of attracting a willing, long-term mate, but his goal is no match for his belief system. His belief system is fueling his process, and his belief system is sticking with habits that work against his goal. He is stuck.

This person may believe that relationships are a waste of time because they always fail in his experience. For example, he could have lived through his parents' divorce at a young age and watched neither have any real subsequent relationship success. This could have imprinted a belief, possibly in his subconscious mind, that good relationships are unattainable. Meanwhile, vodka and porn work successfully to minimize whatever pain loneliness delivers.

His personality, sadly, is composed of those same beliefs driving his habitual behaviors. The biggest predictor of personality, according to numerous therapists, is self-esteem. Though manageable, how people view themselves only partly connects to reality. Whether or not they see a valuable, competent, attractive, and intelligent reflection in the mirror comes from the mind. The bulk of self-esteem consists of what the individuals make up about themselves and believe to be true.

Everyone at some point has encountered that freak with a complete lack of self-awareness. Despite much evidence to the contrary, they confidently act in a way consistent with someone possessing far greater competence. They seem blind to their gross imperfections and assume they deserve a seat at the table with the wealthy, the successful, the attractive, and the popular. Sometimes it is humorous, but funny is preferable to pathetic, and for every self-assured freak, there may be hundreds of self-doubting people feeling worthless who should not.

Those "freaks" are acting with confidence because their internal belief system tells them they are valuable, competent, attractive, and intelligent. Reality, whatever that means, does not matter to them. More often than not, in delicious irony, others eventually start to react to these freaks as if they were valuable, competent, attractive, and intelligent. This means, on some real level, they *become* valuable, competent, attractive, and intelligent.

Conversely, and much more problematic: valuable, competent, attractive, or intelligent people who act as if they are not become worthless, incompetent, ugly, or stupid in the eyes of others. This idea underscores the importance of giving compliments, even if they are complete falsehoods, because beliefs become reality.

There is good news. Regardless of what kind of dumpster fire of a trainwreck anyone's internal belief system is, it can absolutely change. It just requires a little understanding and ownership of the process.

Taking ownership of beliefs, thoughts, feelings, and actions is the first requirement for changing those beliefs, thoughts, feelings, and actions. Beliefs, no matter how entrenched, can change. Religious people become atheists, and atheists become religious every day; nothing is impossible unless one believes it is.

Behaviors create identities, which means identities evolve from the same complex set of beliefs driving self-esteem. There is a lot in that sentence; a second read might help. Behaviors, otherwise known as habits, are manageable by taking ownership of beliefs. It follows that the best way to change a habit, often necessary for growth, is to change the underlying belief.

Beliefs you hold about yourself control your long-term behavior. The idea of "long-term" here is the key, as most people are successful in changing habits in the short term without changing their beliefs. People can quit smoking for a week, eat healthy for a day, go to the gym a few times, or even treat their spouse better for a while. They are simply tricking their mind— the new habits do not match their identity, and whatever change occurs never lasts. As these changes fail to stick, the underlying beliefs are reinforced, making future growth much more difficult.

A great metaphor for the three requirements of behavior change is a golf ball, and it works better for anyone who has ever cut a golf ball open. I may have opened over a dozen golf balls in my youth, disappointing my father for ruining the balls and my mother for ruining perfectly good steak knives, but that is another story.

The reason why anyone would cut open a golf ball is that, at its core, the golf ball contains an incredibly bouncy super-ball. That super-ball comes wrapped in layers of tiny rubber bands (or at least they were in the early 1980s). The familiar white, dimpled shell covers the rubber bands.

The outer shell represents the results of your actions, and humans tend to focus their attention on results. Examples would include a loss of fifty pounds or the acquired ability to play guitar. Results are motivating, and they can absolutely drive growth—they certainly drive goals. However, the outer shell of the golf ball has nothing to do with processes or beliefs; it is just a shell. It represents the outcome or result of any desired growth. While it is very important, on its own, it is useless.

The layers of rubber bands just beneath the outer shell represent those actions necessary to create desired results. The goal of losing fifty pounds requires some process that might involve eating less and exercising more. The goal of learning to play the guitar requires some process that involves getting a guitar, taking lessons, and practicing a lot. The rubber bands beneath the outer shell represent the process.

Too often, people believe their goals, or the outcomes of their goals, drive the actions or processes they use to achieve success. They view the results as their motivation to change their habits and grow. While often effective in the short term, this surface-level motivation is fighting a losing battle with the belief system that has no idea what is happening. The complex belief system that is responsible for behavior, habits, and identity is the core of the golf ball.

28

The bouncy super-ball powers the golf ball as it travels through the air. Without getting into the mechanics of the golf swing, the golf ball's actions during flight use all three components. The outer shell assists in the accuracy of the flight. The rubber bands are keeping the super-ball compressed, and that compressed super-ball magnifies the energy of the strike that initiated flight. They all must work together, and they do. Failing to activate all three levels of true behavior change creates that familiar struggle humans experience most of the time they try to grow: growth gets its power from the belief system, not from the outcome.

Creating identity-based habits from the inside out is not only the best way for people to grow, it also makes the change simple. Consider the chronology: energy is created to fuel a process that results in an outcome. Starting with the outcome is backwards. The process of growth always involves behavior changes, and those habits require a change at the identity level (that is simply a matter of choosing what to believe). At that point, when individuals are consciously choosing what to believe, growth is as easy as falling down or backing up.

So how does one change their belief system? It is a process, it is sometimes complicated, but it is absolutely doable, and not only can that change be permanent, but changes starting in the core improve the odds of success with any potential future growth.

An identity is a product, projected by a series of habits or behaviors. No one is born programmed with certain beliefs. Beliefs form through various experiences and assumptions made navigating through life. The identity projected is usually an embodiment of a collection of an individual's habits, based on their belief system.

If someone is constantly drinking an excessive amount of alcohol, that person would likely assume the identity of an alcoholic. If someone exercises daily, that person would likely assume the identity of an athlete of some sort. It does not matter if the presumed alcoholic possesses no addiction to alcohol or if the "athlete" lacks the coordination to walk and chew gum, much less throw or catch a ball of any kind. Habits embody the identity, right or wrong.

Taking ownership of one's belief system and understanding its importance is the idea. The key process of managing, re-wiring, or re-booting one's belief system misses the cut. This is unfortunate, as this is the most important element to ensuring enduring growth. The good news: it is possible to change beliefs—simply challenging them is the first step.

CHAPTER FOUR

Stop Taking Yourself so Seriously

"Most of the shadows of this life are caused by standing in one's own sunshine."

— Ralph Waldo Emerson

It makes no difference what level of seriousness an individual exudes. Everyone alive and aware of anything would prefer to smile more and stress less. Adults often resent children in this regard, and the famous Irish playwright George Bernard Shaw summed it up perfectly during an interview in 1931. When asked what, in his opinion, was the most beautiful thing in the world, he replied, "Youth is the most beautiful thing in this world—and what a pity that it has to be wasted on children!"

With that, culture witnessed the birth of the popular adage, "Youth is wasted on the young." This profound quote combines wisdom, humor, and jealousy to make an extremely relevant point. It is not hard to imagine what children would do if you gave them pencils and paper and asked them to draw; they would start drawing. If you turned on music and told them to dance, they would start dancing. Asking sober adults to do the same things would likely trigger a negative response from most. Instead of plunging into an activity, adults tend to connect with the logical side of their brain, and most respond with "no" or "I don't know."

There exists a shared fear of ridicule, and potential shame curbs the enthusiasm to live without care as children do. It is deeper than the simple fear of hearing laughter, but not much. Because of that fear, adults abandon activities they enjoy, learning from new experiences, and having fun. For most people, the older they get, the more life sucks—that's a big part of the reason old people resent young people.

When people take themselves too seriously, they choose appearances over new experiences. The fear behind this makes life boring and repetitive, and thoughts of what others think outweigh their own interests. This is the sad part of growing up and probably has a lot to do with the fact that adults can legally consume alcohol in the United States at the age of twenty-one.

In nature, fear exists on an emotional level as a response to some threat in order to keep animals alive; it is a natural reaction to any perceived threat. Fear is not a bad thing; it keeps people on their toes just in case they need to prepare for a real problem. However, the pervasive fear of ridicule has nothing to do with a real or perceived threat of any kind; it is a fear of something that might happen. It is something humans impose internally, rather than something coming from the outside.

Understanding this is huge. It cannot be understated how important managing this is relative to increased general happiness. While self-awareness is not necessarily useless, unfair human tendencies suck the joy out of millions of lives all over the world.

High expectations are not necessarily a bad thing, but expectations are ideals—not determinants—for living, and there is no consistency. For example, people judge others most often for their worst actions, yet these same people judge themselves by their best intentions. This fuels the condescending attitudes that create pressure to be perfect. Humans too often allow expectations to determine how they live. This leads to massive numbers of people taking themselves way too seriously and affording lessor, ignorant peers the power to judge them.

If a man tries to please himself, chances of success are good. As he tries to please larger and larger numbers of other people, his chances go way down, and he eventually pleases no one, not even himself. The blame for this might belong to William Shakespeare, whose famous monologue in *As You like It* begins with "All the world's a stage, and all the men and women merely players . . ."

Because of the fear of ridicule, humans too often treat their actions as performances. How well the "audience" receives the constant performances becomes a source of self-worth. Constantly performing is exhausting, but that does not stop it from continuing.

This concept of life as a performance does get real sometimes. How often is there news of hilarious and brilliantly funny people—some of them famous as a result—taking their own life? Is that a reminder to everyone to never forget that "men and women are merely players"? Some people are just great performers, and the identity they project is that of someone who does not take himself or herself too seriously. It would be wise to remember that all great performers take themselves very seriously—the greater they are, the more seriously they take what they do.

There is a cycle at play here: when people take themselves too seriously, they tend to take others too seriously as well. This leads to an increased value in others' opinions and empowers those opinions with the ability to hurt. This pain fuels the fear of ridicule when, in reality, others' opinions can only hurt if they are allowed.

While no one responsibly advocates against taking life seriously—as everyone has obligations and responsibilities to manage—the practice of taking oneself too seriously produces more pain and disappointment than most people realize. The best defense against this practice is to hold a set of truths with regard to ridicule beyond rebuke. Think of these truths as armor to protect against unnecessary and destructive fear.

Here is a healthy set of potentially relevant truthful statements that could protect soldiers in the ridiculous war:

▸ TRUTH #1 – Stressful worry over problems provides nothing to advance solutions.
▸ TRUTH #2 – Everyone, on some level, is crazy.
▸ TRUTH #3 – It is impossible to change the world by conforming to the expectations of others.
▸ TRUTH #4 – Society, and the people who make it up, stands far from perfect.
▸ TRUTH #5 – Some things in life are unpredictable.
▸ TRUTH #6 – Terminally serious people seriously suck to be around.

No truer list exists. While there could surely be more examples added to this list, these irrefutable truths will serve the exercise well. This is where the ridiculous war ends, and the door to taking oneself less seriously opens.

People find themselves in avoidable, unpleasant situations all the time. Once reality sets in, increasing the stressful nature of the situation only makes things worse. Stress kills people, and though rarely considered suicide, stress is a self-inflicted problem. It is as if, once a problem surfaces, the universal instinct is to make it worse. It is laughably moronic, yet everyone does it—another example of the bullshit instincts of humans. The world would be a better place if everyone knew that stressing out is the least effective problem-solving technique ever and acted accordingly.

Whenever it becomes clear that nothing will change things in an unpleasant situation, the obvious action should be to find humor in it. Stepping away or changing one's perspective from a victim to something of a spectator is often helpful because things rarely prove to be as bad as they seem.

Humans find irony deliciously funny for some perverse reason, and they appreciate those who point it out. Everyone remembers and forgets details of the worst moments in their lives, but no one forgets who made them smile in those dark times. They remember the smile because it helped. When unfortunate situations will not go away, looking for humor is never the worst option, and it can often be the best. This is a learned behavior, and it can be more difficult for some than others, but it might be worth trying to add more joy to life.

Associating with funny people, seeking humor rather than violence or depressing drama for entertainment, purging some of the 24-hour news cycle, and replacing the creation of nasty labels with self-deprecating one-liners are all ways to train oneself to learn to look for humor. It is also important to remember that if anyone ever complains about making jokes at an inappropriate time, it is perfectly fine and normal to admit that humor is a defense mechanism some of the world's enlightened minds deploy in times of stress.

While "crazy" used to be a safe catchall for all mental illness, its use has conflicted with the mores of those enlightened warriors who police the current politically correct culture. Advances in the understanding of behavior disorders, personality peculiarities, and clinical diagnoses have created categories and terms for all of the different subsets within "crazy." There are so many categories and terms today—terms that describe disorders from the very mild to the extremely severe—it follows that every single person alive possesses characteristics of at least one "crazy" diagnosis. Once the idea that everyone is "crazy" is accepted, the political incorrectness of the term loses its power. This creates a shortcut to the final stage of just about any mental health cycle: acceptance.

Acceptance is always the stage that brings the sufferer back to some stage of stability. Acceptance is put in therapists' notes once they see patients taking ownership both for themselves and their actions (this is a nice little hint for anyone wishing to speed up a mandatory therapy process—you are welcome). Based on everything listed here, the reader may have just learned about his or her craziness, even though it is not news to anyone else. It is not a bad thing if it applies to everyone—fingerprints are not bad; nor are toenails, teardrops, or ugly shirts. Everyone has them. Embracing the "crazy" is what needs to be done if taking oneself less seriously, something necessary to grow, is on one's agenda.

It is hard to imagine the world not changing, but humanity is obsessed with the trailblazers who changed the world. Albert Einstein, one of those trailblazers, usually gets credit for the famous quote, "The definition of insanity is doing the same thing over and over again the same way and expecting a different result." While there is much debate over whether he actually created that quote, any investigation into the renowned genius's life would reveal he was never, at any point in his life, in any real danger of conforming to society's expectations.

Society as a whole feels comfort in the status quo, and changes to the existing state of affairs could negatively influence those heavily invested in society's current structure. Therefore, there is a tendency to share that fear with the young by discouraging anything that threatens the natural order and encouraging the virtues of conformity.

Einstein, Martin Luther King, Jr., Nelson Mandela, and Mahatma Gandhi all changed the world by breaking rank with what society expected of them. Every one of them is a positive, inspirational reminder that there are few noteworthy accomplishments achieved by conforming to someone else's standards. It is worth noting that evaluating the impact of the ideas and actions of non-conformists remains important. Adolf Hitler, Genghis Khan, and Karl Marx were famous individuals who changed the world by ignoring the status quo, but they do not share that same universal appreciation as those in the first list. It is hard to get past the fact that they collectively link to almost two hundred million deaths globally. The status quo is not always inherently bad, but questioning it is never a bad idea. The world that today's parents were raised to thrive in does not really exist anymore.

The idea of not conforming dovetails nicely into the obvious truth that society is, has always been, and will always be far from perfect. Notice the amount of time the news devotes to tragic, unfair, and horrible happenings, and compare that to the coverage of inspirational and positive events. Most people would rather not know how exponentially more copies of gossip magazines sell than any works of literature. The ratings of "reality shows" focusing on depraved individuals starved for attention are consistently much higher than interesting biographies or dramatic, thought-provoking dramas worth watching.

Today's society, if evaluated intelligently, probably is not worth any extreme effort anyway. Taking oneself too seriously is, all too often, an action relating to pressures coming from a society rarely worthy of such stress. Choosing to not be a part of something so obviously far from ideal might just be the only prudent option, yet this idea is foreign to so many.

Often the only constant in life is change. No one ever knows what the future holds, and all predictions are simply guesses. In this pattern, it is the human obsession with things impossible to predict that represents the most unnecessary and disappointing agony. While it is impossible to avoid considering what the future might hold, painfully wishing for something to happen or not happen does no good.

If the likelihood of events in the future can seem positive if impacted by certain actions, engage. If not, assume the role of a spectator and prepare for whatever outcome eventually arrives. Things rarely work out as perfectly as people hope, but the ability to react and adapt to changing circumstances will prove far more useful than any amount of stressful planning. It is always preferable to be the light during tough times than to add to the darkness.

In the spirit of light, it is important to evaluate how much enjoyment can be associated with individuals who take things seriously and compare it to the way it feels to be around those who do not. Spending time with overly serious people is rarely enjoyable, and if being the reason others do not enjoy themselves is not a problem to them, then it follows that growth is definitely not their goal.

A friend who can always bring joy to any situation is better in every measure than a friend who has a tendency to make things worse. Someone with the honest, self-deprecating ability to own his or her mistakes will always be welcome. That is not true for the unwavering egoist, incapable or unwilling to accept fault.

Growth is so much more difficult for people who take themselves too seriously. If the goal is successful growth and the idea of it being easy has appeal, own those things that make growth more difficult. Taking oneself too seriously is one of those things—a big one.

CHAPTER FIVE

Get Serious

*"The most difficult thing is the decision to act;
the rest is merely tenacity."*

— Amelia Earhart

With all due assurances, putting the chapter "Get Serious" immediately after a chapter titled "Stop Taking Yourself So Seriously" was intentional. The process of getting serious might be wasted had the two been reversed. Here I will explore the clinical stages of change, which is by far the most serious topic in this book. You should think of this as an adult educational road trip rather than a lecture. The consumption of alcohol—assuming that it is not the offensive habit—is encouraged, if one is into that.

Up until this point, there has been no requirement for any specific potential change. It was safe to still cling to a nebulous story that sounds like growth might be unnecessary. Until now, the reader has presumably existed in what is known as pre-contemplation, where the existence of any specific need or desire for change is required. Up until this point, any reader truly lacking either a need or desire for growth could safely find benefit in continuing this book—but for those readers, the journey should end here.

Perhaps someone, unaware of obvious growth needs, could benefit from the suggestion of this book. Such a recommendation would require delicacy, as some people are comfortably oblivious to their shortcomings. They could take offense to such a suggestion, regardless of how obvious the need is to everyone else.

To those pressing on, two things define pre-contemplation. So long as one is not seriously thinking about changing and they hold zero interest in help of any kind, that individual resides in this initial stage. Occupants of pre-contemplation tend to defend negative behaviors and bad habits, as they claim to not see any problems. They can often be defensive to outside pressures, forcing them to retreat inward, which can make things worse depending on the behavior. This stage, usually riddled with multiple layers of denial, is the toughest to complete.

Fortunately, most everyone still reading has progressed to the second stage: that of actual contemplation, at least. Just like the first stage, two things also define the second stage. The contemplation stage consists of acknowledging a need for change and is marked by the lack of confidence to move forward. The existence of both is essential, as this conflict defines the stage. This stage represents a giant leap toward change, as it embodies that basic concept of ownership, without which growth cannot be possible.

Contemplation is an ideal concept for this stage. While the word itself simply means thinking about something, it can simultaneously refer to reflection, prayer, or meditation. The importance of these multiple ideas is that when it comes to personal growth, it is not always clear where one will conjure the strength required to succeed. Contemplation keeps open all potential options.

In this stage, people are on the fence and weighing their options before making any kind of commitments. It is at this point one considers the benefits of growth and weighs those benefits against the real or perceived costs. It is sometimes difficult to justify the pain with the pleasure, so to speak. While the long-term benefits of change easily outweigh the effort, to those looking from the outside, facing that challenge is often very different for the individual who must pay that price.

For example, deciding to purchase a piece of property worth over a million dollars for less than a hundred thousand dollars would be an easy decision for many people. However, for someone with less than a hundred dollars and no prospective income, the value makes no difference; the price might as well be two million dollars. To that person, the cost is one thousand times more than they can afford to pay, and regardless of the extreme value, moving forward simply is not worth the effort and seems impossible. This is an understanding that people should keep in mind when they become frustrated with others who remain stuck in this stage of contemplation. It is sometimes impossible to understand someone else failing to act when the action is such a no-brainer to them.

What is a bargain to one might be unaffordable to another, and not everyone's contemplation involves identical variables. This is the reality behind the possibility of this stage, sometimes lasting for an extremely long time. Fortunately, this is most often not the case as contemplations usually transition into preparations seamlessly.

The preparation phase begins as one calculates that the desired growth is worth the potential cost. A commitment now exists to make a change, and the research on how to do so begins. These commitments to change often hold various levels of seriousness and formality, and that is okay. The level of seriousness, though important, fails to predict successful change too often. The probability of success lies in where the motivation originates.

Actions conforming to one's core belief system, motivated in part by the knowledge that the change is possible, are exponentially easier to achieve and have a much higher success rate than those that do not. Changes motivated by potential outcomes are immensely more difficult to achieve, and they are nearly impossible to maintain. Ownership and awareness of these truths must be part of this stage, as this is where the necessary actions originate. Any evaluation of the potential impact of those steps must include the consideration of anything that predicts success, and the source of the motivation is, by far, the single greatest predictor imaginable.

In addition to the decision to commit, research characterizes the preparation stage—this book might even be a part of this stage for you. Inevitably, what follows the realization that something must change is questioning how that change should occur. Enthusiasm is always awesome, but resist the zealous urge to jump into action. Patience is difficult sometimes, but moving directly from contemplation to action is a recipe for failure. Any growth, large or small, will undoubtedly create some kind of lifestyle change, and failing to research and accept what that change will require is bad—very bad.

When ready, the action stage combines excitement, optimism, motivation, fear, and pride into one euphoric blast of dopamine. It is recommended that one does everything possible to make those feelings last—whatever strategies adopted or resources employed, it is now time for commitments to become actions. It is now time to start implementing the steps and using whatever techniques are most likely to make their impactful change become reality.

This stage is usually very short but extremely important. Willpower is essential, as it is during these times of making purposeful efforts to change that individuals run the greatest risk of regressions or slip-ups. Strength again comes from awareness and ownership of this fact as the individual re-evaluates the steps taken. Flexibility is often necessary, as the real world often delivers unexpected external pressures. Great strategies to improve self-confidence and to help deal with surprises might include short-term rewards for various accomplishments, internally analyzing progressive behavior changes, and possessing an openness to receiving help or support from others. Once the initial success is achieved, people will then move to the final stage, that of maintenance.

The goal of initiating impactful change often feels as if it is accomplished right away, but growth requires a series of progressive goals. A weight loss goal of losing a hundred pounds safely is impossible right away, but the goal to change one's diet, exercise habits, and routine is attainable almost instantly—that instant success is the action stage.

Growth is dependent on the ability to avoid any actions that could derail one's early success. Growth is dependent on maintenance, the fifth and hopefully final stage. Maintenance is the last stage of growth if, and only if, another stage—that of relapse—never occurs.

The maintenance phase, characterized by those inhabiting it constantly reminding themselves about how much progress they have made, is very important. It is normal for those in this stage to tweak the rules for their lives and learn new skills to deal with life. They are aware of and honest about situations capable of derailing their growth. They maintain awareness of their worthwhile and meaningful journey, and they practice patience in the struggle to turn new habits into second nature.

Successful change is possible, and owning the process improves the odds of success much more than hoping something happens. Getting serious about growth involves understanding the stages and putting them into practice. A commitment to the stages of growth all but guarantees success, and soon it becomes apparent that changes are not just possible; they are easy. The first time a child rides a bike is often a painful, frustrating experience for everyone involved. Every professional cyclist experienced an ugly first ride, but what if every ride after that was some type of personal growth? They would be giants—giants possessing the knowledge that growing is easier than riding a bike.

PART II
START
BACKING UP

"I was thirty-two when I started cooking; up until then, I just ate."

— Julia Child

CHAPTER SIX
Take Inventory

"The simple act of paying attention
can take you a long way."

— Keanu Reeves

In 1963, Matsusaburo Yamaguchi of the Japanese Yamaguchi Electric Company invented the back-up beeper. Most people are familiar with the repeating tone that most large commercial vehicles emit as they switch into reverse to warn unseen passersby. (It is very possible that as a sixth-grader, I spent time in detention for suggesting that one of my teachers should invest in such a device to use whenever she walked backward.)

In any event, the back-up beeper often alerts others to the process of backing up, even if the driver has taken inventory of their surroundings. For a driver, before a vehicle backs up, steps are taken to ensure safety because backing up is more dangerous than driving forward. Even before sitting behind the wheel, recommendations include the driver walking behind the vehicle to ensure the area is clear, especially if there is a possibility of children playing nearby. Drivers should then check and adjust the various mirrors within reach; remaining mindful that relying solely on mirrors can result in blind spots and cause accidents.

After the inspection of the vehicle's rear and adjusting the mirrors, then the driver should start the engine, and only with the driver's foot on the brake. The driver's left hand belongs at the twelve o'clock position on the steering wheel—this is the only driving situation where the driver should ever grip the wheel with only one hand. The driver's right arm should stretch across the seat, and both eyes should be looking through the rear window as the driver's foot slowly releases the brake pedal.

All pilots go through a list of preflight instructions with their airplanes. It makes sense that such instructions exist with space shuttles, heavy equipment, tugboats, and even rickshaws. Regardless of the vehicle, the driver must take inventory of everything relevant to any journey prior to its beginning—and especially before backing up.

Taking inventory, in a personal sense, can be a simple but necessary process. The best way to accomplish such an inventory would be to answer some series of life-exposing questions. The questions can act as a pre-growth checklist or a way to gauge the importance of making a change. Every individual is different, and no two people grow the same way. Losing weight is not always healthy and drinking alcohol is not always bad, for example— therefore, taking some kind of self-inventory should be the first part of any significant process, regardless of how many times it has been done before.

Suggestions for self-inventory questions should include queries into one's overall sadness or gladness. In most cases, honest happiness should indicate that radical change is far from urgent if needed at all. When these questions produce answers, it might be a good idea to uncover the source of these feelings.

Another beneficial concept to explore would be that of freedom. In the sense of defining freedom as the opposite of trapped, feeling free would surely be a good thing. In another context, freedom could equate to loneliness or boredom, which could be quite negative. This is another example where understanding what one is feeling is just as important as why, as it determines whether the answer is good or bad.

Other questions could gauge one's contentment, stress level, ability to love, or feelings of security. It is also important to honestly assess feelings of trust, turmoil, or regret, as well as have a clear awareness of the abilities possessed to heal, let go, and move on from pain. The most important knowledge for any individual is the knowledge of self.

Is this life an example of balance? Alternatively, is there an expectation to move from one dramatic episode to the next? Are the relevant people in one's orbit trustworthy? Do others deserve resentment or forgiveness? These are all great self-inventory questions.

What also matters is the ability to look in a mirror and the discernment of whether that reflection is favorable and why. Only the individual can decide to influence their world or let it dictate their lives, which comes down to setting goals, creating standards, and establishing boundaries, if necessary. The steps of an inventory can be painful, and that is okay—this just means that such an inventory is overdue.

Life has difficulties, and it is crucial to be able to see those things worthy of appreciation and identify those things that could and should change. Taking things for granted can be just as destructive as failing to take advantage of opportunities to grow. The self-inventory process is just as much about seeing the good as it is about seeing the bad: it shines a light on self-love—or its absence.

Taking inventory is a process, and just like any worthwhile process within one's control, simply going through the motions is a disservice and a waste of time. Taking ownership of the self-inventory process sets the tone for growth and all of the related subsequent steps. When it comes to making positive personal changes, the most important information is not in a book—it is locked inside the individual's head.

Humans are not equipped with any process or roadmap for learning about themselves; that knowledge simply emerges through multiple experiences of trial and error. Highly inefficient and hardly scientific, the knowledge of self bases itself on extremely incomplete data. What other options exist? Every individual is unique; no two people share the exact same genetics, experiences, and abilities. There can be no expert on what makes a unique experience.

It takes time to learn about the self, and the quest can never be complete, but it is well worth the investment. The more people know about themselves, the better they are at making decisions, living their lives, and visualizing the futures they desire. Proper self-inventory can enable the individual to use energy more efficiently by aligning habits with core beliefs, saving so many steps.

Learning about the self is sometimes surprising, as people are rarely who they think they are. The most effective way to initiate this type of learning is to focus the self-inventory process on two things: experimentation and assessment. People often struggle with their purpose, which is unfortunate because understanding their "why" gives both direction and meaning to life—it helps to make decisions by focusing on core beliefs.

The self-inventory's effectiveness is a thousand times more productive when the proctor is clear about purpose. Purpose drives individual needs, desires, preferences, and tendencies, and it sheds light on style, strengths, and abilities. People gain confidence from others they trust, from repetition and success, and they are held back by fears, unhealthy habits, and ignorance. All of these things must be a part of a complete self-inventory, and an awareness of purpose simply provides clarity to the process.

The self-inventory can be as long or as short as necessary, but it must include certain things, things that every person interested in growth must learn, and that starts with purpose. The self-inventory must consider energy needs, productivity, values, and motivations. It also needs to understand learning style, habits, natural strengths, personality, intelligence, confidence, and fears. This often takes work, but it is like an open-book test—you already have the answers; you just need to come up with the questions.

CHAPTER SEVEN

Visualize What You Want

*"The harder you work . . .
and visualize something, the luckier you get."*

— Seal

Numerous writings exist professing that the practice of visualization on its own can change a person's life. While that may be possible, the act of mindfully imagining a specific positive outcome prepares the brain to accept success, even when success was unlikely. Further, by consistently repeating that same mindful imagination, one can convince the brain that the unlikely is not only possible but also likely. When the brain feels that something is probable, millions of subconscious actions start falling like dominoes, and some of those actions can tip the scales in favor of the desired outcome. Proper, believable visualization leads the individual to experience the emotions or feelings as if the visualization was reality.

A lot of how the human brain works is unknown, but it is not a complete mystery. Breakthroughs occur every day, and discoveries are commonplace in the world of psychology. It is also important to pay attention to notable outcomes in life. Everyone knows if something was a failure or success, but many fail to take the time to find out why. Those who study the minute details of the process of a particular failure—replaying the different actions taken in their head to discover recurring trends—are creating their own breakthroughs. This represents the most effective strategy for avoiding the same result in the future. However, people should be just as interested in what led to their successes as they are when they review whatever led to their failures.

Anything honestly visualized can become a reality—it can. The key word here is "honestly" because honesty forces the individual to remain inside the realm of the possible. There are countless notable examples of individuals who have accomplished unbelievable things, and they all credit some form of visualization. The truth is that it usually also takes a lot of hard work, time, and focus, but picturing the positive outcome does seem to have a positive impact on the process.

Skepticism is common, and likely healthy, but there are some real benefits to visualization. So long as the process amounts to more than a replacement for actually working in some way, the idea begs the question, "Why not?" If the actual power of visualization equates to only a fraction of what its disciples feel is true, then steps necessary to do so correctly are well worth the time and effort.

Honestly, true visualization is much more than the simple act of imagining great things. Research has shown that vivid mental imagery can have a huge impact on how people implement changes in their lives. People are born with various levels of an infinite number of talents, many naturally blessed with a talent to imagine positive details vividly. These individuals experience increases in energy and momentum, two prerequisites to constructive action. Also understood is that navigation is easier when one can "see" the destination, which is a shared benefit.

Everyone possesses the skill to picture things unseen, and this basic ability represents an example of fluid intelligence. Fluid intelligence includes those skills not learned through education—like memory, discernment, and reason—which work across all cultures. Unused fluid gifts decline from lack of use or with age, but awareness of this concept today can be extremely helpful in training them.

Just as humans exercise their bodies, they also exercise their minds. This important training, not really accomplished through education, represents an enormous opportunity to help everyone grow. The goal of education is to amass knowledge, experiences, specific skills, and understanding to use in life. Training fluid intelligence, which links directly with creativity and innovation, often involves changes; changes include unplugging from technology, escaping comfort zones, and avoid routines.

Concerning visualization, there is a required awareness that every action or creation begins as a thought. Everything ever done exists first in the doer's imagination, which is reassuring, as it shows that visualization is already happening in every mind. Improving or managing this process simply requires awareness of this idea, and this awareness can initiate a deliberate meditative contemplation. If one is going to do something anyway, there is no reason not to do it well. The idea of mental rehearsal is not new, and there are easy exercises to develop and apply the powerful skill of visualization.

In therapy, a simple exercise involves showing someone a photograph full of details, something they have never seen before. The exercise requires scanning the picture to memorize as many details as possible and, with eyes closed, recreate the image mentally. The instructions are to include as much detail as possible into that mental image, including colors, objects, background, or imperfections.

After an extended period (several minutes) of focused visualization, the eyes are opened. Every detail is compared to the mental image, paying close attention to any differences, like birds missing from the sky, inaccurate colors, or freckles missing from a face. The exercise, repeated at least twice with the same image, usually results in an increase in detailed memory of the image. This exercise, repeated with additional pictures, represents a simple rehearsal to improve one's visualization skills.

To step up the exercise, one could examine a three-dimensional object, like a stapler or a set of keys, and imagine the details as the object rotates in their mind with their eyes closed. Creating a mental image of the unseen portion of the object flexes the ability to create images unseen by using available information. It can be even more helpful to examine the same object with eyes wide open and imagine it moving and interacting with other objects in the same area.

Another helpful exercise, useful after mastering the others, involves imagining an ideal location full of detail. This mental image must include every aspect and feature, just like in the previous exercises—and once the complete scene exists, the

58

architect of the scene appears in the location. The vision should include sights, sounds, smells, temperature, and the reactions of all the different elements of the scene to the new presence. Every effort to make this scene realistic is helpful; it should at least look like a movie, and at best, it should feel like a real memory.

To enhance the effectiveness of the exercise, another person joins the scene. It could be a lover, a rival, or a random stranger; it does not matter. The goal here is to imagine interactions with the other person, both good and bad. This practice forces the mind to predict outcomes and to experience the feelings associated with those outcomes as if they have happened.

The more vivid the picture, the more attainable it feels. Studies exist that confirm this idea. When athletes visualize making a shot, a catch, a throw, or a kick in their sport, the likelihood of their success increases. Taking this idea to the next level, visualizing an alarm buzzing earlier to get in extra practice, visualizing working on form, or visualizing the feeling of the ball on one's fingers as it leaves the hand will collectively make dramatic improvements and increase success even more. The more steps detailed in the vision that relate to actions, the closer the goal comes to becoming a reality.

Most people with any sort of fear of public speaking have heard the suggestion that they should imagine the audience wearing only their underwear. While this could create a host of other distractions, potentially worse than a fear of public speaking, envisioning the audience in their underwear is absolutely a form of visualization. A more contemporary suggestion to the same problem, employed by consultants, coaches, and therapists, would involve the speaker vividly imagining their speech executed flawlessly through an audience member's eyes. The vision should include the audience's positive reaction or applause at the conclusion. This strategy has consistently produced increases in confidence, reduced anxiety, and improved delivery. If done correctly, this single exercise can absolutely eliminate the fear of public speaking permanently.

It is similar to learning to dive into a swimming pool. People, some of them grown, have tried unsuccessfully to simply dive headfirst into a pool for years. They want to do it, but right before they take the leap, they bail out and enter the pool feet first—painfully slapping their belly on the surface of the water—or remain on the ledge. Some parents have actually held their children by their ankles and dropped them into the pool headfirst to get them to overcome the hesitation.

Something changes to a person's belief system instantly when they execute their first headfirst dive: they now know that it is possible and that they can do it. The fear is usually gone forever.

Visualizations can have varying levels of detail, and awareness of this is important. The more detailed one's conception, the more specific emotions of that desired state are felt at the neural level. By vividly imagining a first-place finish in a race, a runner can actually experience the dopamine-infused joy of actually winning. Chasing that joyful feeling creates focus and motivation that work toward making the result actually happen. Clear mental images—the more vivid, the better—work like an outside force guiding the individual toward their goal. These images also prepare the brain to accept success as an inevitable outcome.

Another reason conscious visualization can be so important rests in the fact that human brains are constantly working, even when it seems like they are not. Unconscious visualizations, controlled by the subconscious mind, rarely stretch the individual.

The subconscious mind gets its direction from instinct, and that usually involves the mindset of protection.

Basic instincts exist to protect humans from threats and potential pain, including the pain of embarrassment, disappointment, and failure. The idea of keeping oneself safe often contradicts any plans for experiments, improvements, or growth. Ownership and awareness of the visualization process, giving great emphasis to vivid images of success, are crucial in changing anything.

Conscious and purposeful visualization is an effective way to reduce stress—this is especially true for those whose schedules require setting specific times to do things. Summoning the discipline to take time out of a busy day—even just for a few moments—to create a detailed vision of something positive equates to meditation. In that short time, the mind can empty and fill with a sense of relaxation simply not possible otherwise. Add to the relaxation vivid mental images of a desired outcome or state, and that mass of daily stress building up inside the body and mind must start all over.

Focus, an essential part of any personal growth, improves anytime someone clears his or her head. Choosing the idea of some success and creating a clear picture of what that looks like forces out all of the fragmented subconscious noise the mind carries around on a given day. The myth of multitasking, the layers of individual responsibilities, and the chaos of reality work together to cloud focus. The process required for properly visualizing an outcome removes everything, clouding focus in a positive way, almost like flushing a toilet.

Self-confidence increases with each success, and this same increase can exist when visualizations are purposeful. Assuming one is not purposefully picturing negative or undesirable outcomes, the optimism gained from positive feelings drives confidence and increases the belief that success is truly possible.

The universally accepted idea that success creates happiness also applies to visualized success. Even if the imagined future is not true, effective visualization causes the mind to react as if it were. When conceptions create joy, the positive reactions inside humans can only strengthen their power. Even if the visions do not happen, anything responsible for increasing happiness is encouraged by the mind.

Visualizations, in addition to delivering joy, can inspire as well. Few things are more inspirational than the reality of a goal achieved. Given the improved focus and added self-confidence attributed to both success and the image of success, it becomes clear that inspiration can absolutely come from within. In fact, sharing extremely well-imagined visualizations can actually inspire others.

Taking inventory of some of the benefits of visualization, it does not take long to realize that improving the self by reducing stress and gaining self-confidence is huge. These upgrades not only make the person happier but immensely more attractive to others. Internal increases in focus and happiness are contagious, as others can share these feelings, and nothing attracts others more than the ability to inspire. It follows that focused, self-confident, happy, inspirational people, not burdened with stress, have better relationships—they do. Proper visualization absolutely improves relationships, mainly because it improves every single aspect of social behavior.

Visualization is not a secret; people use it all the time. In 1990, Jim Carrey was a struggling comedian. He wrote himself a check for ten million dollars, and, dating it 1994 for inspiration, kept it in his wallet. In 1994, he earned that ten million for his role in *Dumb and Dumber*. He claims to have used visualization constantly throughout his career.

As a young aspiring bodybuilder, Arnold Schwarzenegger vividly imagined his body transformed into that of Reg Park, the legendary bodybuilder from England. As he built up his physique, the change was expected. He claimed the vision was clear in his mind, and he just needed to grow enough to complete it. Schwarzenegger had convinced his mind through visualization that his ideal outcome was possible before there was any real evidence to support it.

Actor Will Smith jokes that he convinced his mind he was an A-list actor long before he ever became one. He still claims that he always was at the top of his profession—it just took a while for the rest of the world to know what he knew. Smith is fond of sharing a particular Confucius quote whenever asked to describe the secret of his success: "He who says he can and he who says he can't are both usually right."

Intentional, vivid visualization does not replace hard work, drive, focus, and determination; nothing does. Carrey worked on his performance and style, Schwarzenegger trained endlessly, and Smith stretched himself as an actor and a performer. Success of any measure is rarely an accident; it usually requires hard work, drive, focus, and determination. Visualization helps to fuel those things.

CHAPTER EIGHT
Give Excuses a Voice

"Ninety-nine percent of the failures come from the people who have the habit of making excuses."

— George Washington Carver

Humans are simple creatures, known for three things. They can regulate their own body temperature, they are skilled at manipulating objects with their opposable thumbs, and they constantly rationalize their behavior. Every other action is just a subset of those three.

The rationalization pillar holds a place in the big three because of the simple reality that any intelligent non-human would marvel at the fact that humans spend more time rationalizing their actions than actually taking action. While it is usually important to consider options, variables, and consequences before engaging in any significant action, those considerations fail to describe the main sources of rationalization. The gross majority of people's self-justifications fall into two categories: excuses and reasons. The problem here is that humans confuse the two.

By definition, reasons are causes, explanations, or justifications for actions or events. Reasons explain the surrounding uncontrollable variables, and they imply that fault is accepted. Reasons, typically given when one human is describing an event's circumstances or actions, possess no intent other than to share accurate information. Any justification put forth as a reason is open for judgment.

Excuses, by definition, are causes or explanations put forward to justify a fault or offense. Created with the intent to either blame someone else or absolve oneself of accountability, excuses become obvious, as they rarely conjure any ownership or solution-focused action. The best way to tell them apart is to see excuses as self-justifications or alibis and reasons as honest explanations or clarifications. A reason illustrates a communicative act, while an excuse appeals to authority—and sometimes that authority is within.

Parents often justify their actions to their children by simply saying, "Because I said so." In their view, they have no obligation to explain their actions to their children, and that makes their response a "reason." Out of fear of some form of punishment, children will often describe a litany of unrelated and related facts when explaining their actions. They have every reason to depict themselves as blameless and hope whatever explanation they give persuades their parents not to assign accountability. Regardless of its effectiveness, this would be an example of an excuse.

If someone invites a friend to go running, and the friend declines because of a broken leg, that would likely be a reason. If they decline the invitation because they "didn't have time," that is probably an excuse. Often there is a fine line between offering a valid reason and manufacturing a well-orchestrated excuse.

For a reason to hold water, there has to be zero possibility for success with an action or event, excluding any workaround in which accomplishment remains possible. This is where the individual's belief system and thought process comes into play. It is never good for one's "reason" to be exposed as an excuse— the resulting transparency illustrates one's actual lack of priority regarding the action or event. It also undermines that person's credibility and displays a perceived lack of integrity.

It is far better to face reality before the instinct of self-preservation kicks in. Confident conversations relaying facts related to an action or event, with no attempts to deflect blame, are fine, especially when they include some takeaway or future solution to prevent any future problems. Conversations require a voice, and effective dialogues are always honest, intentional, rational, and constructive. Excuses result from an impulse to deflect blame, and they are a part of every individual's makeup— they do not simply go away.

The best strategy is to give excuses a voice and let them participate in that internal brainstorming process that should occur before explaining any action or event. The single most effective tool to controlling the impulse to make excuses is the simple act of saying those excuses aloud. It is amazing how much easier it is to distinguish between reasons and excuses when exposed to the light, so to speak.

The extra step of preparing is huge in determining if an explanation is necessary because it could be the explanation is just an attempt to sugarcoat a lame excuse. If an individual is at fault for something, growth cannot occur without ownership. Giving a voice to an excuse is another example of backing up.

Understanding the hazardous fine line between an excuse and a reason is essential, and the safe bet is avoiding both, but that is not always possible. It is vital that the explanation passes a few simple, easy to remember steps.

Before getting into exactly how to navigate these murky waters, a certain amount of reflection is necessary. One must determine if an explanation is necessary or just an attempt to sugarcoat a good old-fashioned excuse. To make this determination, a few questions (asked aloud) about the potential reason are useful:

▸ What impact does sharing this have on the outcome?
▸ Will failing to voice this result in moving forward incorrectly?
▸ Will this just serve to shift the spotlight?

If it sounds like the third question is the driver, then it is merely an attempt to avoid responsibility, and the explanation is an excuse. If no solid reason exists to clarify, then resisting the impulse to add anything at all is the correct call.

With the decision made that there is a need to clarify what exactly caused a failure because the information is that important, attention to how it is presented becomes crucial. This means there is zero need for qualifiers. Prefacing an explanation with things like, "I don't want to sound like I'm making excuses, but . . ." or even the seemingly innocent, "Just so you know . . ." ultimately sends the wrong message. It is best to jump right into the relevant, important information.

The biggest step here, and in this entire book, is to apologize at this point. It is counter-intuitive for humans to say they are sorry, which is exactly why it is so powerful here. Regardless of what exactly happened to get to this point, the story remains the same. Things did not go according to plan, and missteps occurred for whatever reason.

This does not need to be anything complex. It just needs to come out before providing any added background information. It demonstrates ownership by accepting responsibility for whatever led to the event or action, even if there were other factors. More than anything else, this detail makes ownership clear, and it shows everyone involved who is focusing on the solution. An apology also makes it clear that any extra details are meant for clarity and context, rather than any attempt to point fingers or shift blame.

Whenever people find themselves in a place where an action or event has created a problem, most people unconsciously fall into the process of sheltering against fault, even when the problem has nothing to do with them. People, both those unwittingly sucked into the uncomfortable mess and those who dove in confident they were free from fault, all share the same goal of escape: they often look around for someone to fall on their sword.

Someone needs to end this, and whoever does it is the hero, especially if that hero's hands are intentionally full of the problem's blood. Someone needs to transition back to the ordinary and create a "let's move on" statement, and that statement should simply involve a commitment or a short strategy to avoid the same issue in the future. The person who steps up is the winner here, and many people miss this opportunity to win.

When excuses have a voice, their purpose and lack of value are exposed. The aforementioned problem-solving steps of determining necessity, avoiding qualifiers, apologizing, and moving on become second nature when excuses have a voice. Problems are a constant in most events and actions; most often, what actually happened pales in comparison to how those affected react.

There is a real need to filter content when people communicate, which is painfully evident (and sometimes hilarious) when unfiltered comments escape in public. While I may struggle with the concept of sifting out the inappropriate when addressing others, even I can see the need to screen some thoughts. This necessity does not exist, however, when communicating with the self. Softening external messages is an important part of communicating in the real world, but when done internally, it is lying—and lying is almost as bad as creating excuses.

The exercise of saying excuses aloud, a simple trick one should probably do alone, removes the excuses' reasonableness. When excuses are exposed, facing reality becomes easier. Facing reality puts things into perspective, and perspective eliminates the need to provide excuses.

Most everyone reading this book has access to clean water and electricity, for example. Education to the point of literacy is an easy assumption, and, compared to previous generations, access to information and other people is magical. Most humans today live in climate-controlled dwellings, have access to healthcare, and live free from many threats of danger, and these blessings are all good things.

When excuses have a voice, especially in the context of such a safe and comfortable existence, they really sound pathetic. Unless, of course, they are not excuses at all. "Excuses" stated aloud that do not sound pathetic, do not shift blame, and lead to solutions are constructive, clarifying, and helpful reasons. Reasons are honest and helpful parts of any process that leads to growth. Excuses are dead ends.

CHAPTER NINE
Own and Manipulate Reasons

"People don't buy what you do; they buy why you do it."

— Simon Sinek

Assuming a strong grasp on the concept of reason, in contrast with the idea of excuses, now exists, the path to strengthening, understanding, and managing reasons should become clear. The reasons some people grow, as well as the excuses others give for not growing, come from within. That is not to say that these motivations are predestined at birth, because they are not.

The connection between reason and action is rarely visible on the surface, and as a result, many people assume management of either is impossible. This could be laziness or ignorance, and it really does not matter which, because the consensus on both is negative. Effective, positive change, regarded by most as hard work, relies on motivation. The strength of the motivation behind the change offers a far better predictor of success than the actual work itself.

Whether the struggle is internal or belongs to someone else, anyone who has experience with overcoming substance abuse understands the role motivation plays in recovery. There are many treatments available, and they run the gamut from light, suggestive counseling to extreme therapy where one loses liberty. The best predictor of success is rarely the expense or the quality of the treatment; the individuals who succeed at recovery are properly motivated. When and only when the individual is ready will the treatment work.

Rehabilitation from addiction, obviously, is much more complicated than simply deciding to recover. However, absent an honest internal decision to embrace sobriety at some level, treatment can be a colossal waste of time and money. What makes the process so painful for loved ones is the inability to understand how the resulting benefits of recovery could fail to motivate. In reality, those needing treatment usually wish to be better; they even try. Unfortunately, their internal belief system is failing to align with the benefits so obvious on the surface.

The most effective way to begin such a recovery is to discover what internal beliefs or reasons are in conflict with the external motivation to recover. This is the best time to give excuses a voice, as hearing the excuses is sometimes the only way to discover the reason. Once discovered, internal reasons are manageable, but so long as they remain buried, reasons will defeat motivations every time. When reasons and motivations align, anything is possible.

This does not only apply to substance abuse recovery. Unmanaged reasons and belief systems can sabotage weight loss, relationships, work improvement, productivity, willpower, decision-making, and more. Missing any opportunity for personal growth is unfortunate, frustrating, and debilitating. Not only is the personal development unachieved, but also the subsequent failure has real potential to undermine confidence.

Is the internal reasoning, existing within everyone, manageable? The short answer is yes, but some will find this easier to do than others will. Everyone's belief system is a series of stories written in the first person; life, some believe, is simply a process of creating as many of these stories a lifetime allows before "The End."

The ability to change a belief system lies in one's ability to edit their stories. Some people are resistant to editing their stories, regardless of how wrong those stories may be. This is evident in a failing small business that refuses to cease the parts of their business that lose money. Often stronger than clear, obvious facts to the contrary, belief systems can refuse edits out of pure stubbornness.

Most negative, limiting, and un-motivating reasons have links to deep-seated beliefs from stories people continue to repeat to themselves. When the stories of life move from being some objective account of experiences to being repetitive mantras, where the individuals dictate who they are and how things work out, the reinforced takeaways are usually negative. These negative stories—based more on what one can't do, what always happens, and what never happens—exist to support the negative. They include "I never win," or "This always happens to me." Everyone has heard it, and most everyone has said it.

And that is okay; the point is awareness. The idea of managing anything begins with taking ownership, and ownership is only possible with awareness. That sentence might deserve a second reading; it is that important. The relevant actions required to change those internal reasons are not complex, but they all must occur, so one must trust the process.

Initially, there needs to be an active reminder that people write their own stories. The writer must then read the work and find where the story makes broad statements inconsistent with any supporting facts. The next action is to fact-check those unsupported statements through the lens of self-appreciation rather than self-deprecation. The final, and most important step, involves saving the re-write and deleting the previous version. It would be wise to remember these actions if it becomes clear that tweaking the narratives of one's belief system requires extra effort—it likely does.

Everyone likes things to be easy, and while some things are unnecessarily difficult, the process of managing internal reasons involves reading, writing, fact-checking, re-writing, and deleting, in that order. There remains some good news, as there are a variety of hacks that can be utilized.

One such hack involves discovering a specific surface motivation that seems to work. Inventory the times of greatest and least motivation, and be sure to examine this with as few preconceived notions as possible. Awareness of the ability to control motivation is required, and simply doubling up on those things providing the most motivation can improve the odds for success. It is also useful, sometimes, to revisit the past and evaluate times when motivation was easier. Discover what was different, and that could lead to a quick fix.

Another shortcut deals with one's attitude. Choosing one's attitude is not against the rules, nor is it impossible. Motivation, already established as something that comes from within, can improve with minor adjustments to perception. Moving from negative to positive can be extremely helpful. Instead of viewing success positively and failure negatively, decide to enjoy the process and embrace coming up short as an opportunity to continue toward success.

One other simple trick involves changing focus. It is possible to minimize any negative noise coming from internal belief systems by shifting attention to the task. Instead of thinking about all of the work involved in a rehab process, which allows the mind to conjure up thoughts of becoming overwhelmed, one can strengthen the connection between the process and the results. The increased focus can help minimize the impact of any unhelpful thoughts.

Other hacks include connecting with existing beliefs when setting goals, understanding the purpose of the goal, and working to be present every step of the process. It requires far less energy to construct goals around beliefs than the other way around, assuming there exists room for growth. When the purpose of any goal is clear and understood, obstacles tend to shrink. Presence in the process increases the likelihood that our progress will follow the goal rather than some internal negative perception.

Regardless of how one plans to manipulate the reasons driving growth, ownership of the process is an absolute prerequisite of success. Ownership always requires awareness, and awareness allows for proper planning. It always helps to visualize success, and nothing feeds motivation and enjoyment like rewards. Certainly, the rewards from success are obvious, but any process that rewards each milestone is helpful. A collection of small steps will cover a vast difference, and learning to enjoy the journey helps.

The reasons people achieve things or fail to do so are usually the same. Understanding the system that drives reason is powerful, as this is how people learn their reasons affect their actions. That understanding becomes even more important as people learn that they can absolutely manipulate them by owning their reasons.

Manipulating one's own story, and ending the passive (and often negative) storytelling for future reasoning, is a superpower. Most people do not even understand this process, and of those who do understand it, most are unaware that the core reasons for our actions are manageable. Taking control of this aspect of life can definitely make personal growth a constant occurrence for anyone.

CHAPTER TEN

Get Stupid

"Whenever a man does a thoroughly stupid thing, it is always from the noblest motives."

— Oscar Wilde

So far, in this book, the reader's arsenal has increased with multiple tools required for personal growth. There is an exploration into what growth actually means and a lot of time spent on seeing the various barricades capable of derailing that growth. Of course, the idea of challenging beliefs sees some crucial investigative and provocative light. After exposure to a masterful study of taking oneself too seriously, the reader hears a call to get serious.

The process of taking inventory sets the mood for the reader to grasp the complex and important notion of visualization. The unique proposal of giving excuses a voice enables the study of manipulating reasons.

It is almost time to grow. Before the actual concept of growing, however, there is one final trick, which may be especially useful to those interested in growing in some sort of competitive sense, like sports or business.

In reality, the material covered in the book so far is enough to spark some amazing growth. The truth is that the information here provides a huge advantage to readers over those not-so-fortunate souls who have failed to secure a copy of this masterpiece. One would be well within their rights to simply stop now, skip the remaining chapters, and grow on their own, but why? It makes much more sense to simply finish the book and not have to spend the rest of time wondering how it ends.

A secret used by many successful business people is the idea of under-promising and over-delivering. The problem created by promising the moon and the stars to prospective clients is that those clients expect the moon and the stars as a result. They will surely be disappointed when the copy machine jams, the new car makes a noise, or deliveries are not instant. Setting expectations, a lost art in contemporary communication, prevents multiple future problems that typically have nothing to do with the promise, product, or service. The importance of the quest to gain commitment overtakes any critical concern over potential future disappointment.

When someone promises overnight delivery, and it takes two days, a customer might be lost; but when a delivery, promised in "less than a week," takes two days, a customer is elated. It is the exact same two days. Nothing good comes from setting optimistic expectations, especially when they are potentially not sustainable. Most successful people get this.

The idea of keeping expectations low is behind this chapter's theme of getting stupid. There is no better way to reduce external outlooks than to impersonate an imbecile. The idea is quite liberating, actually. No one expects much from those considered incompetent, and whenever the inept accomplish anything correctly, they receive accolades.

A solid suggestion to anyone absorbing this book's contents might involve keeping the information quiet for a while. Waiting until others notice a change will have a far greater motivational effect on the reader, and sharing information about implementing a newly-learned strategy will diminish the impressive effectiveness of any growth.

The smartest people in the world listen more than they talk. Most people are familiar with the quote about it being better to "keep one's mouth shut and be thought a fool than to open it and remove all doubt;" if all one does is talk, how can that person learn anything new?

The earliest relatable examples in one's life of acting dumb to get ahead probably became obvious in middle school. There were always children who were too cool for school: the kids who rarely paid attention, were often in trouble, and seemed to enjoy disrupting the learning process for everyone. Most of these students were dumb, but some of these little devils were not. For the most part, teachers hated these children and gave them just enough of a positive grade to advance to the next grade, usually out of fear of having to deal with those disruptive assholes the following year.

Anyone purposefully wasting opportunities has either no sense or possesses an evil plan to get ahead that mere mortals cannot possibly understand. Wasting education not only disrespects their parents but every individual in the world who did not have the same opportunities. The bottom line: they are either dumb or evil.

There are three obvious reasons for getting stupid within this strategy for growth. The easiest reason would include the fact that no longer is one considered a threat. In any competitive setting— be it business, politics, or sports—smart strategies universally include eliminating threats. Those colleagues not seen as threats not only avoid constant attempts by others to undercut their success, they often receive help in the form of advice, protection, and information. The rivals focus their attention on threats, and this paves the way for success.

A second reason for getting stupid involves the aforementioned under-promising and over-delivering idea. The feelings others have about performance link directly to their expectations. No one expects much from stupid people, and these low expectations typically equate to increased success. Increased success fuels confidence, leading to even more success; it is always beneficial to surprise on the upside.

Stupid reason number three is all about happiness. Internal and external pressures can become widow makers. High levels of stress cause things like depression, anxiety, heart disease, obesity, sexual dysfunction, hair loss, acne, rashes, or problems with the colon—none of that sounds happy. Stupid people are more likely to be stress-free and experience exponentially more happiness than smart people experience.

Acting stupid comes easier to some than others, and the smarter they are, the harder it is to dumb down. Focusing on weakness and avoiding proficiencies simplifies the process. A rocket scientist who is constantly sharing high risk, improbable stock market tips (assuming that such investments are not a second area of expertise) to Wall Street types would serve as a useful example.

Resisting the urge to boast about accomplishments, victories, and success is important when one is getting stupid.

Braggadocios are the most hated creatures on the planet, and they receive the same treatment as any other threats. Constant conflicts, stolen ideas, and missed promotions plague the hated. The best strategy to employ when getting stupid is to collaborate whenever possible. Replacing the "I" with "we" creates a positive sense of teamwork and shields any knowledge, skill, or hidden talent with the group effort.

There exist numerous ways to appear stupid, but some stand out. The most obvious is to dress younger; someone in their forties should dress like a twenty-five-year-old, and someone twenty-five should dress like a high school student.

In the 1992 film *Leap of Faith*, Steve Martin's character Jonas Nightingale, a bogus faith healer, explains why he always dresses so well. He explains that he, as a con man, always needs to dress better than the mark. Most people advise others to dress well or dress up. That advice flies in the face of anyone seriously attempting to get stupid. While looking younger does not necessarily create a stupid facade, no acquired or applied knowledge will ever defeat the appearance of a lack of experience. Looking younger, on some level, manages expectations and projects a lack of proficiency.

Another tip to help in the stupid journey involves the art of speaking. The best tactic with vocabulary involves never using half of it. Making it a goal that every conversation sounds like a first grader on a playground talking to a teacher could help. Placing "ummm" in most sentences cannot hurt, or always ending sentences with "you know?"

It helps to downshift during conversations and avoid quick, witty statements. Slowing down the conversation creates instant assumptions of stupidity. An excellent tactic involves mirroring the other side, which involves restating what they just said in the form of a question. Mirroring is great because it requires zero thought, but it puts the conversation back in the other person's court. It also alerts them to a high likelihood of stupidity, which is the ultimate goal.

Constantly smiling is another trick that works wonders; smiley people are universally associated with the slow members of the population. Smiling also releases oxytocin, which reduces stress and anxiety.

Another great stupid tip involves posture. Good posture projects threatening confidence and athleticism, while a slumping posture almost creates invisibility. People tend to think less of those they do not notice, and a sloth-like posture rarely ignites any serious fight or flight reactions.

The last tip involves sharing knowledge. When someone answers every question as if they possess no earthly idea as to what the answer could possibly be, others assume he or she is useless. Correct, thoughtful answers typically trigger follow-up questions and future queries. This not only works against the goal of looking stupid, but it also invites time-wasters into one's orbit. The smart answer to all questions is this: "I don't know."

When people realize someone possesses a high level of knowledge, expectations rise. Managing or lowering expectations, after all, is the goal in getting stupid. Besides, there is nothing easier than acting ignorant.

While this entire chapter reads tongue-in-cheek, the amusing instructions do serve a purpose: they occupy the mind with a host of random, thought-provoking ideas capable of inspiring unconventional actions. This chapter might not be as stupid as it appears—or is it?

PART III
GROW

"I am not afraid . . . I was born to do this."

— Joan of Arc

CHAPTER ELEVEN
Set Goals

"Setting goals is the first step in turning the invisible into the visible."

— Tony Robbins

In 1953, Texas A&M's football team—fourteen years removed from its 1939 national championship—won only four games, and Coach Ray George resigned after three disappointing seasons. The Aggies' new head football coach, Paul Bryant, was convinced the players were weak and improperly coached. He decided to take his roster of over ninety student athletes to a small Hill Country campus in Junction, Texas, and hold ten full days of brutal three-a-day practices. The region, experiencing both an epic drought and a historic heatwave, provided the seclusion Bryant sought.

"I've never seen a team this bad," Bryant, not known for mincing words, said of his new team. "Half the players are smaller than monkey cojones; the other half are slower than smoke off shit!" The new coach explained that the team goal was to complete the military-style training, and he promised those who survived would become what he considered football players. The coach did not allow water breaks, began practice before dawn, and did not stop until the sun went down. The players would sweat away ten percent or more of their body weight, bunked in tents, and had no electricity.

Only about thirty players finished the camp. All defectors, dismissed from the football team, cited either illness or disgust at the unsafe conditions. The players who survived represented the university on the football field in 1954 and played every single game against teams with rosters over twice as large. Those who endured accomplished the goal set by Bryant before camp.

The Texas A&M football team, full of what Bryant considered "real" football players, only managed a single victory all season in 1954. For Bryant, the man who would later set the record for all-time coaching victories, losing nine games in his first season with the Aggies did not change his feelings. He later admitted regret for the unsafe conditions, as some of his players left Junction due to heat-related health concerns, but he definitely believed at the time that his camp was necessary.

What is the takeaway from the story of Bryant's camp in 1954? The audacious goal of surviving ten days of hell, only to produce the second-worst season in school history, had to undermine the notion of setting goals.

It undermined nothing to Bryant. Before taking the job at Texas A&M, Bryant had spent eight seasons as the head coach at the University of Kentucky. Before Bryant, Kentucky had never played in a bowl game and never finished a season ranked in the top twenty-five. Under Bryant, the Wildcats were ranked by the Associated Press in seven of eight seasons, and they played in four bowl games, winning three. He knew how to create a winning football team.

Bryant would coach the Aggies for three more seasons, winning twenty-five of twenty-nine games with top ten rankings in each of those seasons. His fourth season, his last with any Junction survivors, saw his team start the season 8-0 and earn a number one ranking. That season earned him the head job at his alma mater, the University of Alabama, and the rest is college football history.

The reason for the drawn-out football example is to illustrate that there are many types of goals. It is a fact that people who set goals are almost three hundred percent more likely to achieve significant results than those who do not. Goals are important—and that is obvious when you consider how many hundreds of books exist on the topic—but goals in the context of growth have some prerequisites.

In this book, you have already identified what growth is and understand what could prevent it. With the core belief system exposed, I have directed and changed the focus of seriousness concerning growth. This book explores the idea of taking actual inventory and touches on the ability for one to not only perceive the current situation but to visualize what growth looks like. The enhanced understanding of reasons and excuses prepares you to learn to take ownership of your entire situation—and, ultimately, manage it. There is even a lighthearted consideration of enhancing stupidity as an option for boosting success.

Goals, with respect to the approach presented in this book, remain a crucial part of the process. Successful growth is impossible without goals, as goals exist to define success; there is no other way to measure the changes.

One of the most basic, and subsequently overused, formats for setting goals is the SMART system developed in 1981 by George Doran. SMART is an acronym for specific, measurable, achievable, relevant, and time-bound. The SMART goal system can be an excellent test for any goal to ensure its strength.

Goals can never be too specific, but they can definitely be too vague. Metrics must be available if the goal-setter has any interest in measuring his or her progress. The attainability test helps the goal work as motivation rather than discouragement. Questioning a goal's relevance is essential, especially as it relates to one's overall purpose. The earlier definition of goals as "dreams with deadlines" underscores the importance of an ending—one either accomplishes the goal or does not.

Setting goals in the context of growth can be tricky. There needs to be a perfect balance between rigidity and flexibility, an expectation of success, and an exit strategy. Life happens; unexpected variables materialize all the time, and inflexible goals run the risk of becoming impossible and useless—but when goals are relaxed too easily, motivation evaporates. Even when it is unlikely, actually expecting success maintains the enthusiasm to continue the work. If a football team's goal is to have a winning season, and there are only eleven games, the team must do something after a seventh loss. An exit strategy provides a path that will at least offer some objective to finish the season.

Within the concept of growth, it is important to understand that there are four different kinds of goals and almost twice as many categories of goals. The types of goals, defined by how long they can take to achieve, serve different purposes. Understanding the differences can help determine how many goals are possible at the same time.

The goals that take the longest to achieve are lifetime goals. They can take anywhere from a year to an entire lifetime to complete. These goals require the most visualization, they must align with one's core beliefs, and they involve the individual's real and perceived identities. Lifetime goals that are unrelated to the setter's values have almost no chance at success. If that fact fails to discourage the goal, it is time to back up.

Earlier in this book, the idea surfaces that ownership of one's belief system makes changing it possible. That process remains a requirement if any lifetime goal conflicts with one's system of beliefs. Backing up is not a waste of time in this process, but moving forward with goals that possess zero chance at success is pointless. Anything worth doing is worth doing right.

Lifetime goals for a twenty-year-old will usually look different from those for someone who is forty and even more so for someone who is sixty. It is unusual for these goals not to change over time; they just do so at a glacial pace. It is probably wise to review lifetime goals twice every decade or so. These goals dictate one's master plan and serve as a gauge to compare other types of goals to determine alignment. These goals exist more to create the bigger picture rather than to dictate the specific steps and actions required to get there.

Lifetime goals answer questions like:

▶ What future accomplishments will one's obituary list?

▶ How large and/or close will one's family be?

▶ How much success does one expect?

▶ Will future generations benefit from one's actions?

▶ How many regrets are acceptable?

There are more examples—too many to count—but personal, honest answers to questions like these create the foundations of lifetime goals. These questions force people to confront their purpose, which is fine. These questions expose people to their core values, which is fine. These questions also have a tendency to create bucket lists, which are also fine.

Understanding one's purpose is helpful; awareness of one's core values is crucial. Ownership of the process, and the understanding that anyone can change these things, might be one of the most liberating ideas ever. Creating a list of accomplishments or activities to experience before death, science suggests, adds quality years to people's lives.

The second type of goal, known as a long-term goal, resembles a lifetime goal in that it can provide a blueprint for success and keep other activities on track. What distinguishes a long-term goal from a lifetime goal is a lack of flexibility and a time limit. Long-term goals require information like specific costs, required actions, and time commitments.

While they can be as specific as wanting to invest a hundred thousand dollars in the next five years, they can also be as vague as wanting a legacy focused on acts of kindness. There is a human tendency to overestimate that which is possible in the short term and underestimate potential accomplishments in the long term. A person probably cannot build a fence around a large lot in a day, but that individual likely prefers those odds to those of learning a new language in a year, even though the latter is doable.

Short-term goals are the third variety of goals, and the idea of "short" is relative. These goals could certainly take a long time to accomplish. Usually grouped together with other short-term goals, these work together, or in sequence, to assist in attaining either a long-term or a lifetime goal. The goal-setter is aware of the relationship, and the entire process works if and only if the goals align with that person's belief system.

A lifetime goal could be to retire someday with a million dollars in savings. A long-term goal would be to save a hundred thousand dollars over the next ten years. A typical short-term goal might involve paying off high-interest debt and halting any future overspending: a change of habit. This illustration should shine a light on the fact that these goals, working together, have a much higher chance of success than they have alone.

The fourth and final type of goal, known as a stepping stone goal, represents the specific actions required to achieve the larger goals. These targets usually represent the steps needed to transition between the other related goals. In the above example of saving money, a stepping stone goal might involve creating a budget, opening a savings account, or brewing one's own coffee.

Money goals are great, and they can help make other goals possible, but it is also important to have relationship goals, health goals, and spiritual goals. The real magic is when multiple lifetime goals align, and all of the supporting goals work together. This often happens naturally, but ownership and awareness of this process are extremely helpful.

There are half a dozen rules one should apply when it comes to setting goals. The first and most obvious requirement here is that goals must be consistent with the goal-setter's values. The second rule involves setting objectives within one's control, and while individuals have control, a goal to have no rain for the next month, for example, violates this tenet.

A third directive involves ambition and the idea that if one works toward an amazing, fantastic goal but fails, the result is likely an improvement. Setting a goal to save a hundred dollars every month is easier than committing to save a hundred dollars every week, but if the latter goal is set and the goal-setter falls short, it is still likely that the smaller monthly goal will be exceeded. The idea with rule number three is to think big. Inspirational author Norman Vincent Peale's quote sums up this rule the best: "Shoot for the moon. Even if you miss, you'll land among the stars."

The fourth rule deals with time. It is important to ensure there is enough time allocated for the goal to succeed. The art of positive visualization describes the fifth rule: acting in a manner consistent with one who has every expectation of success will defeat all of the negativity coming from the outside. The final goal reminds the goal-setter to manage risks; everything worthwhile comes at some cost, and awareness of the risks is at least as important as knowing the reward. It is also worth noting that managing risks does not mean avoiding risks; no one ever accomplishes goals that were not set, regardless of risk.

Most people agree that goal setting represents an important activity in any fulfilled life. Awareness of the different types of goals, and the rules for setting them, improves their quality and strengthens their impact. Setting goals is an absolute prerequisite for growth, but there are others.

Strong, well-thought-out goals, if executed properly, can and will result in accomplishments that one should celebrate. Nevertheless, intentional growth involves much more than setting and achieving goals. There is more to do, and that window of opportunity, when you can simply walk away, has closed. You have now prepared, backed up, and started acquiring the tools needed for growth; it would be counter-productive to step away at this point, as there is so much more to understand.

CHAPTER TWELVE
Prioritize This Life

*"The key is not to prioritize what's on your schedule,
but to schedule your priorities."*

— Stephen Covey

In November of 1918, Germany officially surrendered to the Allied Nations, effectively ending World War I. This conclusion frustrated a young American officer named Dwight Eisenhower, scheduled to deploy to Europe just before the surrender.

Instead of heading to war, Eisenhower gained an appointment to Command and General Staff College, where he graduated first in his class. He served as a military aide to both General John Pershing and General Douglas MacArthur.

In 1943, with the United States deeply entrenched in World War II, Eisenhower, now having earned the rank of general, was appointed Supreme Commander of the Allied Expeditionary Force and planned the invasion of Nazi-occupied Europe. His campaign, which began in 1944 with Allied Forces storming Normandy's beaches on what we now know as D-Day, turned the tide of the war in the direction of the Allies.

After the Korean War in 1950, President Truman asked Eisenhower to take command of the new North Atlantic Treaty Organization (NATO) forces in Europe. In 1952, leading Republicans urged him to run for president, and he won with the slogan of "I LIKE IKE."

At this point, you may be wondering how any of this has anything to do with growth. To be clear, it has nothing at all to do with growth, but it would be wrong to introduce a great tool named after a man and then assume the reader knows the backstory. Historical knowledge has weakened over time, and that is unfortunate.

Eisenhower, the thirty-fourth president of the United States, had to make constant and difficult decisions every day of his life. Those decisions became seemingly more and more critical with each appointment. Faced with a need to focus on more tasks than humanly possible on a given day, he invented the now-famous Eisenhower Principle, based on his own urgent, important matrix. This matrix, because of its simplicity and effectiveness, helps many people today prioritize life's focus based on urgency and importance.

The idea of applying Eisenhower's Principle to a strategy of growth is an easy way to supercharge a healthy set of goals. The process acknowledges the limitations of focus and shifts decisions to prioritize tasks in a consistent and intelligent way. One must remember that human instincts usually defy logic and rarely help the decision-making process; it is best to remove them from the equation. Proper use of the Eisenhower Matrix reveals which tasks require immediate action, scheduling, delegation, or no action whatsoever.

The process is simple and begins with a complete list of all tasks. For each task, one must ask two questions:

1. Is this task urgent?
2. Is this task important?

On a blank page, one should create a vertical line in the middle and intersect it with a horizontal line, forming four equal quadrants. The top left quadrant, reserved for all tasks determined to be both urgent and important, holds all tasks that require immediate focus—these tasks take precedence over all others. The top right quadrant contains all tasks determined to be important but not urgent—these tasks require scheduling at a future time. The bottom left quadrant houses all tasks deemed urgent but not important—the proper course of action for these tasks involves some form of delegation. The final quadrant on the bottom right gets all tasks determined to be neither urgent nor important—these tasks require no current or future action other than removal from the list of tasks.

QUADRANT ONE URGENT & IMPORTANT DO NOW	QUADRANT TWO IMPORTANT/NOT URGENT SCHEDULE FOR LATER
QUADRANT THREE URGENT/ NOT IMPORTANT DELEGATE	QUADRANT FOUR NOT URGENT/NOT IMPORTANT DELETE

Once this concept begins to feel natural, the time management process clears up, as if by magic. An example of something that belongs in the first quadrant would include completing a tax return before April 15th. An example of a task that belongs in the second quadrant might involve intensifying a workout routine. The third quadrant might hold turning a process into a PowerPoint presentation (something easily assigned to another team member possessing a better handle on the software). The final quadrant is where the tasks that involve correcting incorrect political posts on social media belong.

What comes out of this process would be a to-do list from quadrant one, scheduled events from two, delegated tasks from three, and a bevy of time-wasters flushed from one's mind thanks to quadrant four. The Eisenhower Matrix is a powerful tool for scheduling tasks, but one must remember the goal is to set up tasks for intelligent completion. If there are ever more than seven tasks in a particular quadrant, then one may be spending too much time on scheduling tasks. The focus needs to move toward completing those tasks.

A good habit to get into when prioritizing tasks includes making scheduling every day the first priority. Involving others in this process can defeat the purpose. Ownership of this process is the most important aspect, and allowing outside "schedulers" to dictate the priorities undermines all the work done to establish the relative urgency and importance. This can be hard to do in many situations: sometimes, the rug disappears below one's feet because of emergencies or directives from superiors. If the process must change, it will; and if that happens, one should simply reset, prioritize and schedule again.

By maintaining focus on the matrix, the importance of tasks will simply fall back into place. There is nothing more motivating than the satisfaction of completion, and refusing to get off track is the secret. The two enemies of this process include procrastinating and endlessly deliberating the process; one should set times with deadlines and outlaw the movement of tasks from one quadrant to another.

A last thought regarding the matrix would be to suggest that tasks related to work share space with personal or family interests. If the objectives exist on separate lists, there runs the risk of one list (likely work) being promoted above the other. As motivating as it is to complete tasks, nothing demotivates people more than realizing work has prevented fulfilling obligations at home. This can result in conflict and unhappiness, and in an effort to avoid both, public and private tasks must always coexist on the same matrix.

The idea of prioritizing one's goal-related tasks is usually two-fold: getting things done efficiently and effectively. Tasks accomplished correctly and on time are efficient. Ownership evolves within the schedule-priority continuum; something magical tends to happen. Individual schedulers move from the practice of efficiently prioritizing their schedule to effectively scheduling their priorities. The effectiveness ensures the right tasks are completed. This is an example of subtle but colossal growth.

When one is arranging tasks by importance, the tasks themselves are in control. There is nothing wrong with this, as everyone has obligations and responsibilities beyond their control. One might be surprised to find out that most duties are self-imposed and are of suspect importance. This concept describes the day-to-day execution of activities, and with increased success comes increased efficiency.

Tasks, created because they further one's priorities, indicate that the individual is in control. Priorities, when considered first, dictate the order in which tasks are completed. Their importance, driven by what matters most to the individual, ensures completion. This level of ownership leads to next-level effectiveness.

Efficiency and effectiveness are sometimes mutually exclusive in that both cannot be possible with the same action, and a balance is required. Effective actions are completed, and the desired result is accomplished, and efficient actions occur in the best possible manner. Effective measures accomplish the objective, while efficient measures achieve the best results with the least amount of time and effort.

In a 2020 blog post on www.joyexcel.com, Jayabrata Das explains that being effective means "doing the right things" and producing results, while being efficient describes "doing things right" and not wasting resources. An effective individual produces higher quality results and pursues perfection, while an efficient individual offers quick and intelligent work that meets deadlines.

An excellent, relatable, and real-world example of a deliberate strategy to perform both effectively and efficiently would involve a young, recently married man. Assuming this man's goal is to be the best husband he can be, he has likely educated himself enough to learn that open communication is the single best predictor of success in a marriage. It is also likely that he has figured out that men and women have a tendency to communicate differently. Through his research, this young husband has decided that his first response whenever his bride approaches him with a conversation should be a prepared question.

"Is this a listening conversation? Or is there some problem that I need to fix?" he will ask. An effective listener is listening for some opportunity to provide a solution to a problem. If his young wife only wishes for her husband to hear what she is saying, it is far more efficient for him to listen with the goal of empathy in mind. It is also more effective at improving the odds of a successful marriage.

Both efficiency and effectiveness are desirable attributes in most situations. A healthy tug-of-war between the two demonstrates awareness and balance, especially concerning accomplishing and prioritizing tasks. The takeaway from this should involve awareness and ownership of all tasks related to one's goals. Also desirable is an understanding of the importance and urgency of those tasks, as well as a conscious effort to employ both efficiency and effectiveness in completing them. Growth occurs with every completed task, especially when they align with one's beliefs. Knowing when to focus on which tasks reveals an uncommon awareness and a healthy capacity for personal growth. A prioritized life is a fulfilled life.

CHAPTER THIRTEEN
Demand Accountability

"At the end of the day, we are accountable to ourselves . . . our success is a result of what we do."

— Catherine Pulsifer

In a small city in south Louisiana, there is a large community baseball field. Local recreational leagues have played little league baseball there for decades, and one of the fields in the far back end of the complex butts up against the backside of a residential neighborhood. The left-field homerun fence doubles as someone's backyard fence. As the resident has a large lot, they have collected a few homerun balls over the years.

One day, several decades ago, an underachieving, over-sized pre-teen turned on a fastball and sent the pitch over that fence, over the large backyard, and through a giant window on the second story of the house. As the glass shattered, most of the players and coaches looked away. Some players shoved their faces into their gloves. The batter could not hide his smile as he trotted around the bases. But after he stepped on home plate, high-fived all of his teammates, and returned to the dugout, everyone's attention turned to the direction of the house as a mean-looking older man was walking from his house toward the fence, fast, holding the baseball.

When he reached the fence, he yelled, "Who hit this damn ball?"

The kid's smile vanished, and after every soul in the park turned his way, pointing him out, he raised his hand.

The man angrily screamed for him to come to the fence.

Time stood still as the terrified kid walked through the outfield to the fence. When he got close to the man, he took a deep breath, looked him in the eye, and said, "I hit it, sir, and—"

The old man cut him off and said, "Helluva hit, kid, here's your ball. You make sure you bring it home and give it to your parents. You hear me?"

"Yes, sir," he said. "Thank you."

The smile returned to his face as he proudly walked back to the dugout with his trophy in his hand. He kept the ball and gave it to his parents, but he never forgot how scary it was to walk over to meet the old man at the fence. He never forgot how relieved and proud he felt after he received that ball. Forced to be courageous, he took ownership of what he had done and was aware of the consequences. It all worked out. It is a shame that experiences like that happen to so few young people because there is no way that a kid can ever forget something like that.

One of the best things a person can have is a mirror. This is not so much for vanity reasons; mirrors also represent something missing in the modern world. A mirror is honest, sometimes the only honest item in one's entire existence. A mirror never lies unless it is malformed or broken, and a mirror creates a real-time, accurate, and unfiltered reflection of whoever chooses to look into it.

People constantly hold others accountable—sometimes fairly, and other times, not so much. There is a tendency among humans to credit themselves based on intentions and judge others based on their actions. This tendency is worth avoiding, as it gives the individual an unfair advantage and an inaccurate picture in self-perception. People should use the same standard for the reflection in their mirrors that they employ when they evaluate others. A good, long look in the mirror should be step one to whatever process involves holding others accountable.

All of that being said, the humans who grow the most often become leaders of those who do not. Leaders must hold those in their charge accountable, which is not possible without first holding themselves accountable. Those who must hold others responsible must possess the three attributes for actually being accountable . . . just like the kid who broke the window with a baseball. Those essential attributes are courage, ownership, and awareness.

The idea of being accountable sounds great. In theory, it seems to be the most obvious choice. In practice, however, it can require a great deal of courage. In some cases, circumstances force individuals to be brave. Most of the time, courage takes a back seat to fear, shame or self-preservation. Courage is a decision anyone can make whenever they choose, and it is an essential attribute for accountability.

Being courageous is naturally uncomfortable. Anyone with such an attribute can endure being uncomfortable, and the truly courageous seem unfazed. It requires a lack of fear of consequences, a pattern of selflessness, and a tendency to do the right thing. Courageous individuals appear to operate with a higher purpose. Some people are simply wired that way, but most people need to work to develop courage—and it is possible. One must remember that courage does not mean there is no fear, but rather that one must decide to act in spite of it.

When people demand accountability, positive results only occur to those who actually hold themselves accountable as well. Holding others accountable is often necessary, but not everyone can do it; while courage is important, ownership is more so. Leaders do not waste time blaming circumstances or blaming others, and they see little value in making excuses. They create situations, most of them imperfect, but they always display ownership.

Most people possess a sense of right and wrong, and most people would probably prefer to escape consequences for their missteps—this is normal. Integrity, often defined as doing the right thing when no one is watching, can be given away, but it is often impossible to regain. For one to say, "I thought no one could see me" is rarely, if ever, an appropriate excuse for any sort of shameful behavior.

When things go wrong, the first suspect needs to be that person who resides in the mirror. Truly accountable individuals always question themselves prior to any investigation. They will work to uncover what they could have done differently and then move toward fixing the problem. They are rarely looking to find fault outside of themselves, at least not until they find a solution.

Developing courage and taking ownership when others choose not to is what being accountable is all about. Unfortunately, however, the issue or problem is not always easy to see. Awareness is the third essential attribute of the responsible, and without it, there is often no opportunity to display accountability. One cannot take credit for what one cannot see or does not know. If there is no knowledge of a problem, how could one possibly be accountable?

Ignorance may be bliss, but it rarely looks good on anyone. Sometimes the situations that demand accountability are subtle, and the fact that some people are consistently unaware of problems eliminates them from consideration. If they do not know what is going on around them, they certainly cannot devise solutions. For example, when it comes to meeting expectations, how does one identify success? Can they see it? Do they deliver on their promises? Do they sometimes over-promise and under-deliver?

The simple awareness of the need to hold oneself accountable is necessary. However, awareness alone is not sufficient—one must act on what one knows. This is why absolute accountability requires courage, ownership, and awareness. Exceptional accountability requires uncommon courage, ownership, and awareness.

CHAPTER FOURTEEN
WTF Just Happened?

"After Tuesday, even the calendar says WTF."

— Jess Paris

There was once a college math professor burdened every semester with the task of teaching one remedial course to freshmen, a class full of individuals she deemed to be "not college material." All of the war stories she shared in her retirement involved the bastards from these classes: students, she believed, who actually made her dumber with each forced conversation she shared with them.

One story she shared repeatedly involved a particularly self-righteous and sanctimonious young male student who, to her, lacked not only intelligence but also self-awareness and tact. He consistently entered her office before class without an appointment and shared his plans for spending his inheritance, finding a wife, and owning a variety of profitable businesses. He never mentioned, she noticed, the reasons he apparently could not tie his shoes, wear deodorant, or wait for his turn to speak.

It was near the end of the semester, and out of fear of having this waste of oxygen in her class again, she pulled the young delusional clown off to the side.

"I'm not sure how, but you are very close to earning a passing grade in this class," she explained to the student slowly. "You do need to make a C+ on the final tomorrow, and I have prepared a study guide just for you. Study this and only this all night, and you should be okay, but if you don't, you will fail the class and have to take it again—if they let you back in school."

The student took the study guide and went home without a word. The next day, as the professor handed out the exams, she noticed the young man still nervously studying the material. She told the student to put the study guide away and handed him an exam. She retreated to her desk to work on a crossword puzzle and dream of the Manhattans she would drink later to celebrate the end of this godforsaken class.

Twenty minutes into a two-hour test period, the student handed her his completed exam. He had a look of anger in his eyes as he walked out of the room. She immediately started grading his exam and, within a few seconds, realized that his test was perfect—this D- remedial student had aced her final exam! She imagined this grade would make his day.

Eventually, the rest of the class turned in their exams, and she retreated toward her office. Her least favorite student was waiting at her door, still with a look of disgust on his face.

"You tricked me!" he accused the professor loudly. "I was scared to death, so I studied all night. I studied your study guide, I re-read the chapter explanations, I took practice tests, and I reviewed all the tests we took so far. I didn't go out with my friends last night, I didn't talk to anyone on the phone, and I didn't even sleep," he continued. "I did all that for what?"

Confused, the professor showed the student his graded exam. It had "100 A+" written at the top in red letters. "You didn't just pass; you aced my final," she said. "You can now take your freshman math courses."

The student snatched the test from her hand, crumpled it into a ball in her face, and threw the test on the floor. "Of course I did!" he yelled, still pissed. "That was such a waste of time. Your test was the easiest test I have ever taken. I can't believe I wasted so much time studying for it."

As the student walked away and out of the professor's life forever, she thought to herself, "What just happened?"

When things are so important that schedules are changed, sleep is deprived, and stress overwhelms the spirit, the fact that the truly prepared accomplish these things easily is beyond comprehension. When someone typically unprepared, like the delusional student who aced his final exam, suddenly takes the appropriate steps to succeed, something happens to them when the actual success comes. The brain, conditioned to expect the usual results, interprets the success as an anomaly. The human brain must rationalize anomalies, or they jeopardize the status quo, and this creates reactions that sound like "that was too easy" or "that was just luck."

This happens all the time, and the rationalization—not the previous behavior—blocks the individual from the growth opportunity. The professor fully expected the student to realize that his prior approach to education was incorrect, and he would somehow realize the problem and adopt proper study habits. Instead, his rationalization convinced him that he gave up time and sleep to prepare for something easy.

In reality, the test seemed easy because of how prepared he was. This is unfortunate, but it highlights an oft-missed opportunity. Not everyone is a researcher applying the scientific method to controlled sets of causes and effects; life, unfortunately not universally regarded as a learning experience, provides a constant stream of semi-controlled experiments and their subsequent results. Too many people view the end of school as the end of their education, but reality suggests that education never ends. There are opportunities for growth all over the place, and people waste those opportunities every day, often chasing things far less valuable than growth.

Growth is what one desires it to be. Growth is enlightenment, personal development, progress, and evolving; growth is growth. Most people have a grasp on what they want, but that clarity sometimes only comes with growth itself.

So far, you have also explored the nature of obstacles or barricades to growth. It takes effort sometimes to develop the ability to see the obstacles preventing growth. Often these limits are self-imposed, sometimes they originate elsewhere, and other times, they are not even real. People must know what growth is and develop the skill to identify anything that could possibly get in the way.

Another important step toward growth involves a conscious effort to move from a life of actions related to impulses and based on instincts to a purposeful existence, where actions match belief systems. The challenging notions of what belief systems are and how they change weigh heavy on the transition. The concept of taking ownership over one's belief system should trigger an epiphany in some, as this is new information to millions of people.

The next idea in the journey of preparation involves addressing the seriousness in which one takes himself or herself.

The requirement of understanding and owning self-perception intentionally replaces useless fears of potential ridicule. Only then can one get serious about the inevitable.

Getting serious about growth involves picking a specific change or changes identified as desirable growth. Every part of preparation ends when one begins the process of backing up, the initial actions that lead to actual growth.

Backing up includes the process of taking self-inventory, visualizing specific growth, and even giving nagging excuses a voice. Now exposed to possibilities of owning and manipulating reasons, one receives not only permission but also a roadmap and encouragement to get stupid. All of this opens the door for growing to begin.

All intentional growth starts with setting goals. The goals, now prioritized, and the goal-setters, held accountable, have no option but to move forward. All of this work, preparation, and focus leads a person to the point where change is almost inevitable. The awareness and ownership of all the different parts of the process have steered the change in the direction of growth. In most instances, the only thing left to do is to effortlessly fall back into the desired growth one has been seeking.

The work-required effort is not necessarily easy and comes at some cost. However, the result of all that work will be easy, purposeful growth—but one must not forget that the growth is easy because the process that leads to it is purposeful. Failing to understand this puts a person in the same boat as the student still angry about wasting time studying for an "easy" exam. By this point, you should be looking for growth opportunities and no longer ignoring them.

CHAPTER FIFTEEN
Measure Growth

"Every line is the perfect length if you don't measure it."

— Marty Rubin

In a high school biology class review the day before the final exam, a teacher answered what he thought were serious questions about the human digestive and excretory systems. Not realizing at first that all of the questions were about solid human waste, and the students in the back were laughing uncontrollably, he drew diagram after diagram on the chalkboard, unsure where the confusion originated.

When a question came up about the weight of solid human waste, the teacher finally caught on. He said with a smile that no one really knows, adding that researchers found the smell and the texture too offensive to perform any type of accurate measurements.

One student volunteered to "push through" and actually weigh a sample for extra points on the final. This made the room explode with laughter—the teacher even joined in. Once composed, he offered ten bonus points on the final exam to anyone who could devise a sanitary, non-repulsive method for weighing a sample that would not require manipulating the sample in any way.

The class, comprised mostly of seniors, did have one single freshman, and she alone effectively presented such a method for measurement on the final. She alone earned the ten bonus points.

Her method required a scale capable of measurements as small as a gram and as large as a hundred kilograms. Her proposed process also required a human subject, primed for excretion. The subject would stand on the scale, and the precise weight recorded. The subject would then engage in the process of excretion by depositing only solid waste into a commode. After completing the task, the subject would once again stand on the scale. With that precise weight recorded, the first weight minus the second weight would indicate the waste's precise weight.

The moral of the story is one can always measure crap. This also applies to growth, but much like the bonus on the test, creativity helps. The most holistic method for measuring growth comes through four important steps, easily remembered by the acrostic EACH:

▸ Evaluate goals and progress
▸ Assess success through metrics
▸ Catalog necessary improvements
▸ Help from others

It is almost impossible to revisit one's list of goals too often. The only constant in life is change, and change occurs in all aspects of life, including individual belief systems, values, and priorities. Goals need to adapt to changes, but they can evaporate and become obsolete without revisiting them.

It is not enough to review one's goal. What is necessary is to evaluate goals through the lens of the goal-setter's personal values. This entire process of growth involves, potentially, changing one's beliefs. When people make such changes, they learn right away that the process does not resemble turning on a light bulb. Changes in belief systems can happen over time, organically, and may look like evolution with some unintended results.

Goals set early in a belief system change are at risk of not aligning with the eventual new values. This is all perfectly fine; however, it is important to be conscious of all the changes and be aware of how all the different aspects of growth relate to one another. Revising goals is not evidence that the goals were bad; rather, it provides evidence the process is working.

Revisiting goals is a chance to check up on progress made. Once they have been determined to align with any new values, the quality and quantity of accomplishments become obvious. At this point, one can assess headway and decide if the improvements meet, exceed, or fall short of expectations.

If one's progress is determined as insufficient, it forces the question of why. It is extremely important to determine if any actions require change or any goals need adjustment. Some goals seem realistic enough and specific enough when set, but in practice fall short; there is nothing wrong with this, and it is the reason for the first step in measuring growth—evaluating goals and progress.

The second step involves finding metrics to gauge growth, and this often requires creativity. It is not always possible to measure growth with numbers, but if it is measurable with figures, that is where one starts. The best strategy is to start with the easiest metrics available and work toward clarity. For example, if one's goal were to extend the amount of time they can hold their breath, the obvious measurement would be to count the seconds between breaths. By recording that number and tracking it over a period, the progress becomes data. The data can then populate graphs, charts, or tables that can illustrate progress.

Most people track business success in dollars and cents, and this might be the easiest metric available. There exist countless apps, programs, and platforms to measure money, but what about things harder to measure, the more abstract goals?

This is where creativity helps. It might help look at a goal as a house: comprised of many materials and processes, a new house requires many different aspects to align. A house must emerge from a plan designed by an architect and constructed by a builder. Materials include wood, bricks, concrete, nails, glass, and so on. The building process usually starts with a foundation, followed by some sort of framing, and eventually, walls go up and so on. When construction is finished, the house is ready to serve its purpose.

Goals can be broken down into their different processes, steps, or parts, and those elements can reduce further. The process repeats until the goal-setter has something easily measurable.

The starting question should ask what success looks like or how one knows they have succeeded. Take the goal of getting into better shape, for example. Ignoring the obvious lack of specificity, the goal could mean so many things. It is important to know what success looks like—is it a reduction in weight, increased stamina, better flexibility, improved strength, or lower blood pressure? Getting into better shape usually means something completely different when one is twenty than when one is seventy.

Measuring weight loss is relatively simple, and so is measuring blood pressure, but measuring strength requires marking progress in a weight room with respect to weight lifted and the number of repetitions. The more abstract ideas like flexibility and stamina involve complete ownership and awareness of what those things look like. Understanding one's flexibility or stamina at the time of goal setting, to the extent that it could contrast with what those things look like today, is what is necessary. Understanding the change helps determine if one is moving in the right direction, and it also helps if there is a specific vision of what ultimate success looks like—smaller, measurable aspects of the process provide better information for assessing progress.

Assessing success through metrics can be difficult, but it is only possible if one is aware of the situation at the onset and is able to gauge changes over time. For those things easily measured, the only requirement is an accurate recording of any measurable data at the start. Using the same instrument, if possible, to measure before, during, and after the process provides truer information.

The third step involves cataloging necessary improvements. This is where the previous step's data creates a to-do list for the goal-setter. It is normal for some aspects of growth to progress faster than others, and indexing those elements needing the most attention helps keep the focus where it belongs. It is perfectly all right to set new goals or simply tweak the approach to the existing ones. If a goal to save more money negatively impacts one's credit score, it might force a change in strategy; it is unhealthy for a goal to harm other aspects of one's life. This all requires ownership and awareness of not only the goal but the impact of the actions furthering the goal.

The idea of cataloging necessary improvements underscores the fact that goals need to be dynamic and flexible. The more frequently this step occurs, the more efficiently goals can be achieved. Imagine someone traveling on a series of roads and then taking a wrong turn—the sooner they realize what they have done, the sooner they can reroute, and the sooner they can arrive at their destination.

The final step might be the most eye-opening occurrence in measuring growth, and it requires one to seek help from others, usually from a trusted friend or family member.

Even if one can identify his or her own strengths and weaknesses, an outside perspective is always helpful, especially when it comes to progress. Assuming they are aware of the growth journey, others can often provide insights invisible to the individual, and others can have a tremendous impact by forcing accountability and providing support.

Help from others can also come from professionals: a therapist can help track emotional growth, and a personal trainer can help with fitness goals, for example. Regardless of where the help originates, it is an important step in measuring growth.

When someone can effectively evaluate goals and progress, assess success through metrics, catalog necessary improvements, and get help from others, they can literally measure any type of personal growth. As with measuring crap, creativity still helps, but actively measuring growth increases the chances of success, and having a method makes it easy.

CHAPTER SIXTEEN
Rescue Someone Else

"When you learn, teach. When you get, give."

— Maya Angelou

The late author Robert Heinlein, known by many as the Dean of Science Fiction Writers, published dozens of novels over five decades. In his 1951 book *Between Planets*, the main character, Don Harvey, ends up stranded on the planet Venus, which is currently engaged in a war for independence with Earth. This is problematic, as Harvey is trying to get to Mars but finds Earth-backed currency is now worthless on Venus.

Stranded and broke, Harvey "borrows" money from a banker, who instructs him to pay it forward. It seems to be a small part of the plot, but the concept eventually became the philosophy of Heinlein's humanitarian organization, the Heinlein Society.

The Heinlein Society still exists today and is dedicated to teaching the "pay it forward" philosophy to others. The organization holds blood drives, delivers books to active duty military, provides undergraduate scholarships, and creates free educational materials to assist schools in teaching science fiction works in class.

The idea of paying something forward is the opposite of payback: if a person does a good deed for a second person, instead of paying the first person back, the second person does a good deed for a third person. The process creates a perfect system of good deeds—until it lands on some greedy, selfish loser who fails to keep it moving.

How does this concept apply to this book? It doesn't . . . yet.

The creation of this book began with the idea that personal growth might be unnecessarily eluding a large number of people. The thought held by many that growth only comes with hard work and extreme effort might be preventing numerous people from even trying—that limiting, negative consensus requires some sort of a rebuttal.

This book opens up the possibility that growth is not only possible but, in some cases, easy. If the ideas presented here have been of any benefit at all, the final part of the growth process involves sharing that benefit. This step, the last part of the growth formula, must occur.

This step is necessary, not for the good feelings such actions grant, but for the growth process to complete itself. If this book helps its readers, it is reasonable to infer that it will also help others, and sharing, loaning, giving, or recommending it will likely result in another reader receiving the same help.

Helping others will improve one's mental health by boosting feelings of happiness and positivity, but helping others can also benefit one's physical health. Acts of kindness create warmth, known to produce a hormone known as oxytocin. This hormone releases nitric oxide, which dilates the blood vessels and can reduce blood pressure. Paying anything forward also reduces depression and anxiety, and it can improve relationships.

The ideas in this book force the reader to apply ownership to their situation, be aware of their actions, and take responsibility for their future—this is huge; it would be impossible to understate the importance of these breakthroughs. To complete the process fully, it must continue, and the evidence of the ownership, awareness, and responsibility gained rests in the act of sharing the knowledge with others.

Everyone benefits from growth, and sharing information that could potentially help someone escape whatever has them currently stuck might change their life or even save it. No one really knows what someone else is experiencing, and there is a tendency to show others that things are better than they seem. Opening the doors to growth might be the greatest gift one can give.

There exists a measure of satisfaction with every unselfish act. Something as simple as recommending a book communicates interest to others. Such positive attention usually inspires appreciation and may create a culture of generosity and compassion. It does not take much to change another person's outlook and attitude, and by simply fulfilling the final step in this process, one can change another's trajectory for the better.

The process of sharing this information either begins or continues the cycle of growth, which is powerful. The task of rescuing someone else demonstrates accountability, and by considering the needs of others, one demonstrates credibility. This concept of service to others is sticky and contagious because it makes everyone's lives better, even the person providing the service.

Whenever people pay anything forward, the action stands out—it is a break from the norm. It impresses others and affords things like confidence, respect, and trust. Right or wrong, no one doubts the giver who wants nothing in return. This positive reaction inspires the courage to share more readily, and that is growth in itself.

The fact that personal growth leads to more growth notwithstanding, the step of sharing in the hope of rescuing someone else is self-affirming. Even absent altruism, helping others improves self-image, and that improvement is visible to others. Growth shows, and it looks good on everyone.

These types of activities become part of one's process and can often extend to future generations. The process itself is one of momentum, and stopping momentum is exponentially more difficult than allowing it to continue.

There are an infinite number of reasons to help others, but making it this far in this process displays the ownership and awareness required for growth. That responsible cognizance must spread because once one experiences the satisfaction of real personal growth, the change becomes obvious.

But this idea of rescuing others immediately after liberation is nothing new; it is actually almost ancient. In his brilliant 1841 essay "Compensation," Ralph Waldo Emerson details the need to promote and account for this concept of giving:

"In the order of nature, we cannot render benefits to those from whom we receive them, or only seldom. But the benefit we receive must be rendered again, line for line, deed for deed, cent for cent, to somebody."

Amen.

CPSIA information can be obtained
at www.ICGtesting.com
Printed in the USA
LVHW021040030621
689238LV00005B/330